SIMPLE
COUNTRY LIVING

28 27 26 25 24   1 2 3 4 5

ISBN: 978-0-7603-8540-1

Digital edition published in 2024
eISBN: 978-0-7603-8541-8

Library of Congress Control Number: 2023948262

Design and Page Layout: Tanya Jacobson, tanyajacobson.co
Cover Image: Annette Thurmon
Photography: Annette Thurmon, Kristin Faye Photography, Jessica Mignola Photography

Printed in China

SIMPLE
COUNTRY LIVING

Techniques, Recipes, and Wisdom for
the Garden, Kitchen, and Beyond

ANNETTE THURMON
OF
AZURE FARM

COOL
SPRINGS
PRESS

TO MY SWEET
Ava Rose,

May you always have a love of nature and all of God's creations. Thank you for inspiring me to find joy in the simple things each day.

CONTENTS

Introduction

If someone had told me fifteen years ago that my days would be spent chasing chickens, tending to a garden, and embracing the role of a homemaker, I would have most definitely chuckled. But life has a funny way of surprising us with unexpected twists and turns, leading us to places we never imagined.

As a rapid-response nurse, rushing to Code Blue situations and witnessing people at the lowest points in their lives, I became acutely aware of the alarming state of our collective health and our society's unprecedented levels of sickness. Countless factors around us promote an unhealthy lifestyle: pollutants in the air and water, sedentary lifestyle, and dependence on screens, to name a few. Plus, our food is processed, genetically modified, and full of harmful ingredients like aritificial dyes. Our soil is deprived of essential nutrients, leaving our food devoid of the necessary vitamins and minerals. While working at the hospital, I found myself searching for ways to improve my well-being and that of my family.

Simultaneously, I pursued a side business designing couture wedding gowns. Though vastly different from nursing, it allowed me to express my creativity and experience the excitement of the fashion world. I found myself at events like New York Fashion Week and featured in prestigious publications, such as *Martha Stewart Magazine* and *The Knot*. However, as I delved deeper into the fashion industry and its inherent competitiveness, I realized the pressure it entailed. A wedding dress was no longer a beautiful gown for a special day; it was a symbol of perfection, constantly striving to outshine others. After a decade of designing wedding gowns and seventeen years in nursing, it was time for something different. But what?

My husband and I, with some help from the 2008 economic crash, started to feel called to pursue a new path, away from the noise and a world that seemed more and more fragile and unsustainable. We wanted to reinvent ourselves and reconnect with the basics of life—when families commonly worked the land, derived joy from tending to animals, and cultivated bountiful gardens. A quote from *Country Living*, one of my favorite books written in the 1800s, resonated with me: "The occupation most favorable for character development is the care of plants and animals." I pondered why we couldn't find the same contentment in that lifestyle today. I wanted to explore whether less indeed could be more—less media, fewer screens, less materialism, and fewer distractions.

We searched for years until we finally found a place we could afford—a piece of land with an existing barn. The beauty of the sky on the day we visited the property inspired its name: Azure Farm. We spent the next year building our home and learning to work the land.

I'll be honest: Those initial years were magical but they were also incredibly challenging. Fueled by excitement, we wholeheartedly embraced this new lifestyle. We built more barns and added chicken coops, planted trees, and cultivated our food. We encountered setbacks, losing chickens

to predators and experiencing failed crops. When one of our alpacas died, I seriously questioned our choices. Why did we live far from the nearest store, enduring the hard work of raising our own food, when we easily could buy what we needed there? I questioned my original motivations—why did I want this lifestyle in the first place?

That's when it hit me. The joy I experience living a rural lifestyle far outweighs the hardships. The more I immerse myself in this way of life, the less appeal the external world holds for me. Physically, I am healthier; mentally, I am happier. Recalling the satisfaction of harvesting veggies from our garden helps me weather the disappointment when crops fail. I find contentment without popular television shows. I cherish raising my daughter amid nature rather than in front of a screen. Nature became my source of well-being and its lessons are deeply ingrained in the person I am now.

When people ask about my occupation, I proudly declare, "I inspire others to live a simple life." Sometimes, it takes the right motivation and a gentle push to embark on a different path. And I'm here to assure you that living a simple life is possible and more fulfilling than anything you'll ever experience. Writing this book has allowed me to put on paper the things I've learned and hopefully to equip you with what you need to embrace this lifestyle. It's about making simple changes that profoundly impact your life no matter where you are in life.

This book is an extension of my heart. It's about making simple changes that will profoundly impact your life. Don't be afraid to live differently, my friend. I'm here to debunk that notion in a world that incessantly tells us we need more. True joy can be found in listening to the birds sing as the sun rises, gently tugging carrots from the earth, and making meals together in the kitchen. These things bring about the utmost joy and infuse life with true meaning. And not just in your own life, but also in the lives of your family and friends. Thank you for taking the time to read this book.

Wishing you all the joys this life can bring,

Annette

FINDING YOUR "WHY" *and* SHARING *it* WITH OTHERS

In our fast-paced world brimming with incredible technology and the allure of social media, it's disheartening to realize that we often feel more disconnected and lonelier than the generations preceding us. If you're reading this book, it's probably because you find peace in the idea of living a simpler life—a life that brings satisfaction at the end of the day, where you can witness the tangible fruits of your labor.

It's a desire to escape the bustling city and embrace a smaller community in the countryside where simple living and self-reliance permeate every aspect of life. Because, in the grand scheme of things, what truly matters is to feel gratitude and experience those unforgettable, meaningful moments with those we love. For me, embracing a simple lifestyle in the country has brought joy. Yes, I may feel tired at the end of the day, but I'm immensely grateful for the blessings each day brings.

This chapter takes you from defining why you want to make this change to planning and moving toward your own goals, then to sharing what you've discovered. There's no need to wait to get started.

A LIFE-CHANGING WAY TO LIVE

———

Aside from your desire to live differently, there are several compelling reasons why I believe adopting this lifestyle is so beneficial.

Stress Reduction

Engaging with the earth and getting one's hands dirty has been scientifically proven to release endorphins (feel-good chemicals) in the brain. Excessive screen time disrupts our sleep and elevates our stress levels. I can attest that spending time in the garden, even just pulling weeds, can be incredibly therapeutic after a stressful day. Growing our food and working with our hands are inherently valuable, fulfilling activities that our society too often frowns upon as dirty or dismisses as menial labor. Chapters 3 and 4 of this book highlight all you need to know to garden successfully, no matter where you live. And if you can't garden, that's okay! Even just five minutes of fresh air and sunshine can boost your mood, help clear your mind, and put you in tune with the living world around you. Flowers I used to think smelled the same now smell different. I recognize the songs of various birds and appreciate the morning air. You will find renewed joy in the simple things, and your stress will melt away.

Finding Joy

In addition to finding stress relief by being in nature, finding joy in my work is crucial for my overall well-being. When I worked that stressful job at the hospital, I would find such peace coming home to our farm. Those few minutes outside in the garden and feeding the animals before bedtime gave me peace and calm at the end of a busy day. Even if I had a stressful day or felt I did not accomplish much, I could see tangible changes in the garden from one day to the next and be excited. I believe that by dedicating time to activities such as enjoying nature, growing food, preparing meals at home, and embracing self-sustainability, you, too, will discover more joy in your daily life, regardless of your circumstances.

Food Security and Self-Sufficiency

By embracing this lifestyle change, you will transform your perspective on food and revolutionize your consumption habits. As a society, our food has undergone a significant transformation in the last hundred years. It no longer possesses the same nutritional value it once did. Depleted of essential vitamins and minerals, the quality of our food has suffered due to unhealthy soil and lengthy transportation distances between farm and plate. Consequently, most produce is plucked prematurely, before it develops vital nutrients, only to ripen during transit. Even if it is ripe when picked, produce starts to lose nutritional value once it's removed from the main plant. So, if we are eating food 1,500 miles away from where it was grown, we are missing out on some of its nutritional benefits. Our grocery store shelves contain food laden with artificial dyes, additives, and preservatives. We find ourselves fatigued, in poor health, and longing for change, not always recognizing the link to our eating habits.

Learning to grow your food, obtaining it from local farms, and making food from scratch at home are better ways to provide your body with the nourishment to thrive. Chapters 5 and 6 delve into preserving your food and mastering the art of creating homemade meals. It may seem daunting at first, but once you experience the satisfaction of baking your bread or crafting your pizza, the store-bought versions will pale in comparison. These activities will make you healthier and contribute to your happiness and contentment. I know we all lead busy lives and some of these ideas may seem impossible to fit into your schedule. But remember, this change in lifestyle won't happen overnight. I just suggest you try making one meal at home each week. Don't overthink it, just start somewhere and you will be grateful you did.

The Importance of the Family

Some of my most cherished memories from my childhood revolve around the time I spent at home with my mom. As a homeschool student until seventh grade, my days were filled with valuable moments with her as my teacher. There was a simplicity and joy in those experiences that I wished to replicate for my own family. However, the fast-paced nature of our modern world has taken its toll on family life.

We have become so consumed by busyness that even sitting together at the dinner table has become a rarity in our society. Prioritizing family meals—even once or twice a week—is a small change that can lead your family toward a simpler, more self-sufficient lifestyle. Make this time something special and sacred, even if the meal is ordinary. Chapter 6 suggests a fun way to make setting the table into time for family bonding.

Now that I'm home with my daughter, I realize how important family is in today's world. I wrote this book with that in mind. Each chapter shows different ways to involve the whole family—and friends—in this lifestyle. The activities help us build strong bonds and create a sense of community. They don't have to take up much time, but I promise they are incredibly rewarding and enriching.

In our household, we've implemented a no-screen rule for my daughter, encouraging her to spend time outdoors and acquire essential life skills by assisting me in various tasks. Embracing this lifestyle is a profound choice that led us to a happier family dynamic. No matter your own choices, remember that you don't have to conform to societal norms and expectations. Instead, prioritize the sanctity of the family unit and opt for a simpler way of life. You'll equip yourself and your loved ones with ingredients for happiness and well-being.

TRANSITIONING TO
THIS LIFESTYLE

———

I remember the first time Jared and I talked about moving to the country. We had for years felt called to move out and do something different, get back to the basics of life. But what did that mean? Spending more time outdoors and in nature seemed like the perfect escape from the hustle and bustle of daily life, but I honestly had no idea where to begin. Looking back, I wish I had started living this lifestyle long before we had acres and chickens. Waiting for perfection is one of the biggest things holding us back. We wait for the right time, look for the right house, the right piece of land. We dream of animals at our feet and bountiful harvests each season, glossing over the hard work and potential for failure. As magical, idyllic, and true as this sounds, you do not need all of that to live a meaningful life.

Simple country living isn't a picture we paint in a storybook. It is a lifestyle of fulfillment and working with our hands—oftentimes hard work. It's seeing the fruits of our labor and savoring harvests, and understanding the value of that effort even when some of our crops fail. It's learning life lessons from animals, the way we learned from the unbreakable bond between Milo the duck and his friend "Chicken" (not our best name choice) or from waking up night after night to bottle feed a premature baby alpaca. As

my love for nature grew, my desire to shop for the latest trends faded. I found respite from the chaos and noise the world offered by making simple changes in my and my family's lives.

Here are a few things I do: choosing to make a meal together at home instead of going out to eat, growing my herbs in a pot outside my back door rather than buying them from the store. The term "homesteader" is often used to describe someone seeking to live a more self-sufficient lifestyle. It may sound old-fashioned and off-putting, but I believe any one of us can be a homesteader. It starts with a mindset—there are no rules. You are a homesteader when you remove the clutter, live intentionally, slow down, and become more independent! No matter in which way or where you choose to do it.

Does this mean your life will be easier? Not necessarily. It's a misconception that a simple lifestyle is all homemade lemonade on the front porch while chickens wander through the perfumed blossoms of your garden. It's hard work, but there is so much satisfaction at the end of the day—and that glass of lemonade sure does taste good.

MY HOMEMADE LEMONADE

YOU WILL NEED

2½ cups (590 ml) cold water, divided

½ cup (118 ml) raw local honey

1 cup (236 ml) fresh squeezed lemon juice

2 cups (453 g) crushed ice

Fresh sliced strawberries (optional)

Yield: Serves 4

Instructions

Place the honey and ½ cup (118 ml) of the water in a small saucepan.

Warm over low to medium heat, stirring gently, until the honey dissolves.

Remove from heat and allow to cool.

Add the cooled honey water, lemon juice, remaining 2 cups (472 ml) water, and the ice to a large pitcher. Garnish with fresh strawberries, if desired.

Knowing Your "Why"

Before embarking on a lifestyle change or making a significant transition toward a simpler, more sustainable life, it's crucial to understand the underlying reasons behind your decision. Each person has a unique motive. Take the time to jot down yours.

The reason behind my move to the countryside was simple. I yearned for something different. I had enjoyed the glitz and glamor the world had to offer but it wasn't satisfying. For a few years, I dreamed of a peaceful environment where I could grow food and find solace in the outdoors while caring for animals. I wanted to pursue a life where less is more and embrace nature's blessings. Knowing your "why" will guide you through every aspect of this journey, from initial planning to decision making and day-to-day actions. Understanding your motivations and desires will make all the hard work and effort worthwhile.

Sometimes, homesteading or living a self-sufficient life can be challenging or push you out of your comfort zone. The heartache of losing an animal or experiencing crop failures after nurturing seedlings for months can be devastating, but setbacks are inevitable. In such moments, your "why" will serve as a beacon, helping you persevere and reminding you of the reasons that prompted this change.

Once you have decided to change your lifestyle, I encourage you to immediately start making tangible changes. Don't wait for lots of land and donkeys (although they are undeniably adorable) to begin living the simple country lifestyle. The biggest misconception is that you must start big or have a lot of space right from the start. You

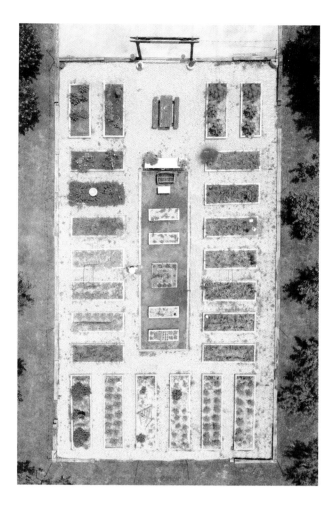

can create your country-living, homesteading, or self-sufficient dream no matter where you live! Analyze your current situation and circumstances. What are the possibilities in your present location? Can you start with a few potted plants or create small garden beds? Is it feasible to keep larger animals or only a handful of backyard chickens? Can you start making some foods from scratch and preserve others for later? Do you wish to have a nontoxic and nature-inspired home? Assess your needs. You can embark on this transformative journey without delay by acting based on your immediate resources. Even the most minor steps contribute to realizing your desired lifestyle.

Dream Big but Start Small

Dream *big* when you envision what you want. Without considering constraints—money, time, and space are no object in this dream—describe your ideal simple lifestyle. Do you foresee a big move? How much land do you have and what buildings are on it? How do you want to use that land? Do you have herds of livestock or just a few chickens, goats, and some bees? Do you have a kitchen garden or fields of crops—or both? How do you envision your relationships and livelihood? Write a beautiful and thought-out vision that if someone hears, sees, or reads, they will catch the vision and want to see it become a reality.

Once you have a vision for the changes you want, but before you make any sudden changes, slow down and start small. Take the time to carefully plan *how* to execute your dream. What time and resources can you dedicate to this new lifestyle? If your lifestyle change calls you to move out to the country, what does that mean for your life and livelihood? The truth is that people want to see a beautiful idea carried out sooner rather than later, and our impatience sometimes gets the best of us. But you need to take the time to plan all that you want to do. Doing so can help you avoid making mistakes—sometimes costly ones—rather than jumping right in and then realizing you ran out of room or dug up the wrong part of your yard.

Whether you are going to live in the same place you do now or you're going to move, familiarize yourself with the area and the landscape. Talk to the locals and neighbors. Get information from the local agricultural office and have a chat with the local veterinarian. Read up as much as possible about the topics you are interested in. Know your growing zone and climate, which will be essential for deciding which animals to keep and which vegetables and fruits to plant. All these steps are necessary to review as you dream big and make a plan. Consider your available resources, time, and finances. In our home, we have tried to save up and do projects only when we can pay for them. Sometimes this has meant waiting a long time to finish certain things. It hasn't stopped me from continuing to do what I can. Keep dreaming, see the vision, and work toward that goal a little each day.

Getting Started (Small)

I am here to tell you that taking a second to slow down will help you in the long run. Once we bought our property, it took years for us to add a greenhouse and animal spaces. And I still do not grow 100 percent of the food my family needs. It can be overwhelming to try to do everything successfully all at once. Choose one or two self-sufficient activities that truly captivate your interest and dedicate your efforts to perfecting them. Over time, things like cooking from scratch, embracing a minimalist approach to technology, or cultivating your herb garden will be learned.

The key is to start somewhere. For instance, consider the art of food preservation—a rewarding activity that can be done regardless of your setting. Even without a vegetable garden, you can begin by purchasing fresh produce from the local market and utilizing seasonal ingredients for canning. Start with one recipe and master it. An excellent option for beginners is pickles! It's an easy recipe (see page 156) that is an ideal introduction to the canning process. Alternatively, you may want to learn how to can your tomato sauce (see page 154) instead of relying on store-bought options.

(I discuss other preservation methods in chapter 5.) As you delve into this process, you may discover that it becomes one of the most enjoyable activities associated with country living.

When it comes to doing things outdoors, building garden beds, planting trees, and such, there are a few things I like to consider before making quick changes.

- Look at the sun: Does it kiss all the ground where you hope to have a garden?
- Which room in your home gets the most sun where you could start seedlings?
- Where will a compost pile work?
- How does the water drain in a big rainstorm?
- Is there a spot you can put a few fruit trees?
- If you want animals, where would animals have space to free range and be safe?

Avoid overwhelming yourself with numerous new endeavors. Instead, focus on mastering a few specific tasks or projects until you feel confident and accomplished. Educate yourself on the changes you want to make. Once you have gained experience and a solid foundation, gradually expand your horizons and explore new possibilities. Take time to absorb and grow your skills and knowledge. This approach not only develops valuable abilities but also nurtures self-reliance and independence. Remember to start small and embrace the joy of gradual progress.

INSPIRING OTHERS

Family and friends were skeptical about our decision to move an hour away from "civilization" to the middle of nowhere. I did experience a sense of isolation at first. But the immense joy and contentment I discovered in our new life motivated me to share pictures of our animals and document our daily experiences. Over the years, I have delighted in hearing stories of people who have embraced this lifestyle, inspired by what we have shared. I firmly believe in the power of our actions to effect change in the world. When we wholeheartedly pursue our passions and live the principles that we advocate, we can rally others into becoming part of our journey.

Create Community

To find your people, lead through example. Embody the life you want others to embrace. Integrate the core values of simple country life into your daily routine, showcasing the immense fulfillment and rewards it brings. Engage in heartfelt conversations where you share your experiences, allowing others to witness the joys and benefits of how you live. Openly discuss how this lifestyle has positively impacted your well-being. By authentically sharing your personal stories and lessons learned, you can inspire others to seek a similar path.

One of the hardest challenges when making a lifestyle change—or attempting most anything, really—is lack of support. Feeling alone makes everything harder, and that experience isn't unique to humans. A unique example of this was when we purchased Buddy the donkey during our first year at the farm. He was young and full of spunk and I naively thought he would be happy with the alpacas and other animals on our farm. But I had not done much research before getting him and I was so wrong. Buddy misbehaved and brayed all the time. He was anxious and in need of a friend. After eight weeks, we brought home another donkey named Chili and it was instant happiness. Buddy's rowdy mischief transformed into days playing and chasing after his new friend.

Fast-forward six years to when we wanted to add geese to our large flock of birds, as they are known to help protect others and alert them to danger. Only one of the eggs we ordered hatched. My daughter named the little gander Gonzo. He seemed fine with the flock and would hang out with the ducks and turkeys and spend time alone in his water trough. Despite him appearing to be "fine," based on previous experiences with having just one animal of a particular species, I wanted to ensure he had friends. So, the following spring, I got more eggs and we hatched six goslings. I cannot describe the pure *joy* on Gonzo's face when, a few weeks later, he saw them for the first time. He ran over, they played and ran around, and the rest is history. He has never been happier than he is as their leader and protector, and his goose friends follow him around all day.

Just like Buddy and Gonzo, you can derive and inspire joy by surrounding yourself with those who understand you. Finding people who share your passion and support your quest for a simpler, self-sufficient life might mean volunteering at a local farm or connecting on social media with people across the country or around the world. Your community is wherever you find and cultivate it. Encourage and guide each other and create opportunities to interact socially, but also to reach out and grow your circle.

Connect Them with Nature

Promote the joy of spending time outdoors and appreciating nature's beauty by connecting those around you to nature. Organize nature walks, hikes, or camping trips that allow others to immerse themselves in the tranquility and peace found away from the noise and distractions of the city. Nature-inspired gatherings are a fun idea worth embracing. For instance, you could plan seasonal activities like visiting a strawberry patch (for more details, refer to chapter 2). Encourage individuals to incorporate nature into their homes, as well. It can be as simple as using fresh fruits and herbs to infuse your home with natural scents and not artificial air fresheners.

Dinner in the Garden

At Azure Farm, we love to enjoy an outdoor meal together. Select a picturesque area in your garden that can accommodate a dining table and chairs. If you don't have a garden, it can be a patio, a cozy corner, or a grassy area with a picnic blanket. Consider the size of your guest list and ensure everyone will be comfortably seated. Create an inviting atmosphere by illuminating the space with string lights, lanterns, or candles. Decorate with natural elements, such as flowers, wooden serving boards, and woven placemats. Tailor the menu to the season and your guests' preferences. Highlight the flavors of the garden. Incorporate local produce, herbs, and edible flowers. The key to a memorable garden dinner is attention to detail. Create an atmosphere that allows your guests to relax and savor the beauty of nature. Don't forget to enjoy the process yourself and cherish the time spent with loved ones.

STOVETOP POTPOURRI

YOU WILL NEED

Peel of 2 lemons

¼ cup (12 g) dried lavender or ½ cup (24 g) fresh buds and stems

5 or 6 fresh sage leaves

4 cups (944 ml) water

Instructions

In a medium pot, combine the lemon peels, lavender, fresh sage, and water, bring to a boil, and let simmer over low heat for several hours. Add water as needed throughout the day. This method allows you to infuse your home with natural scents, avoiding toxic air fresheners. It's an easy and enjoyable way to bring the essence of nature indoors.

Teach Sustainable Practices (and Emphasize the Benefits)

Educate others about sustainable practices that align with a simple country lifestyle. Teach them about organic gardening, composting, raising backyard chickens, or preserving food. By sharing practical skills, you empower others to make positive life changes. Tell them about improved physical and mental health, stronger community bonds, and a reduced ecological footprint. Discuss how it can lead to a more balanced and fulfilling life away from the consumerist culture of the modern world. I believe the benefits are ones your friends and family will see and feel just by speaking with you and visiting your home.

Share Simple and Nature-Inspired Gifts

I love the idea of my lifestyle permeating all I do, from how I eat to how I spend my time. When it comes to gifts, I want them to reflect who I am and what I represent, and I've included so many gift ideas in this book. Canned goods are a perfect housewarming gift. Homemade granola or bread is also a big hit. Personalized gifts, such as pressed-flower frames with a family member's favorite flower (see chapter 4), are meaningful and memorable. Let's not forget that fresh flowers are always a good idea. If you're looking for another simple handmade gift, try the flower bath salts (see page 26). They combine the calming effects of a salt soak with the beauty of flowers—and you can dry the flowers yourself.

DRIED-FLOWER BATH SALTS

Make sure to use flowers that weren't treated with pesticides before they were dried (see page 144 to learn how to do the drying). You can store this in a cool, dark—and dry!—place for up to 18 months. You can tie a ribbon around the top of the jar and even add a dried lavender sprig for decoration.

YOU WILL NEED

1 cup (300 g) Epsom salts

1 cup (300 g) sea salt or pink Himalayan salt

½ cup (115 g) baking soda

½ cup (1 g) dried rose petals

½ cup (24 g) dried lavender buds

½ cup (14 g) dried calendula buds

½ cup (12.8 g) dried mint leaves

16-ounce (473 ml) glass canning jar with a tight-sealing lid

Instructions

Thoroughly mix all ingredients in a large bowl.

Pour the mixture into an airtight glass jar and label it with the contents and instructions. Use 1 or 2 handfuls per bath.

Relax and enjoy!

CULTIVATE A LIFE WELL LIVED

———

I hope this chapter inspires you to embark on the journey of cultivating a well-lived life. Remember to be patient and grant yourself grace, as transformation takes time. It's okay to stumble and struggle, whether it's keeping your tomato plants alive or learning to preserve your own food. The key is to keep moving forward; eventually, you will find your rhythm in a slow and simple life.

The beauty of a simple existence lies in finding delight in the little things and drawing strength from the power of community. Embrace the opportunity to connect with nature and discover the profound joy of getting your hands in the soil. As you cultivate this connection, not only will your life flourish, but your family will also thrive.

So, let us simplify our lives, immerse ourselves in nature's embrace, and share the abundant joy of cultivating life with those who surround us. You will not regret it, friend.

The NATURAL *(and* NATURE-INSPIRED) HOME

There truly is "no place like home," as the saying goes. It's the familiar scents and personal touches that make it so unique. No matter how many breathtaking places I've visited around the world, my heart always yearns to return to Azure Farm. Particularly after navigating the challenges of the pandemic, I've come to cherish our home as an oasis amid the chaos. During this time, I discovered a profound appreciation for nature's inherent rhythms. I find solace in the blooms of our Bradford pear trees signaling the warmer weather in spring. The captivating sight of golden and orange leaves cascading in the fall brings me joy. And in winter, as the garden slumbers and conserves its energy for the forthcoming spring, I find renewed energy for the coming months.

Over the years, I've discovered various ways to infuse nature into our daily home life, from engaging activities to incorporating seasonal foods into our meals. I decorate our living spaces by bringing elements of nature indoors, adding a touch of its beauty to our surroundings. Taking it one step further, I've consciously embraced a cleaner and more sustainable lifestyle by choosing nature-friendly products. Living in a home where we use fewer toxins and allow the fresh air in is so life-giving.

I am confident that by allowing nature to inspire your home life, you, too, can experience the same profound joy and contentment that I have. Join me on the pages that follow for some of my favorite ways to embrace a more natural home.

CREATING FAMILY TRADITIONS
AROUND THE SEASONS

———

Creating family traditions around nature has become a part of what we do because being outdoors is such a big part of our lives now. I believe it has given us a stronger bond as a family.

I love having something to look forward to at certain times of the year that is special and unlike any other. For example, making chive blossom vinegar is one of my highlights each spring. An act as simple as cutting blossoms

CHIVE BLOSSOM VINEGAR

YOU WILL NEED

A mason jar

Fresh chive blossoms

White distilled vinegar

Instructions

Rinse the blooms and remove the stems.

Pack the blooms into the jar and fill with vinegar.

Cover the jar and store in a dark place for 2 weeks.

The vinegar will turn a purple color with a delicious scent.

Discard the blooms and it's ready for use!

from the garden to create a unique vinegar can be fun and something to look forward to. If you start incorporating some of these traditions, you'll also foster a greater appreciation for the environment and the world around you. Here are a few traditions you can incorporate into your home life each season to get you outside and in nature. The end of this chapter includes activities your family can do together each season. Let these activities inspire you to create your own traditions around the things you love most about each season.

Spring

Since moving to Azure Farm, witnessing the emergence of new life each spring has made me realize that this season, rather than fall, is my favorite. Spring, with its blooming tulip bulbs, longer daylight, and profound sense of rejuvenation, has an enchantment all its own.

The garden's thriving crops, like peas, carrots, and cabbage, depict abundance and vitality. The arrival of spring brings forth a symphony of chirps and quacks as our new baby chicks and ducklings fill the brooder. In the greenhouse, we sow summer seeds while the garden receives its share of attention with the planting of spring seedlings. The alpacas are sheared, shedding their winter coats, and the fruit trees get fertilized, ensuring a bountiful harvest to come. It is a beautiful time of year and the perfect season to do something outdoors.

What to Take to the Berry Farm

- Sun hats
- Baskets for those yummy strawberries
- Drinking water (it can get hot doing all that berry picking)
- Closed-toed shoes (the fields can be muddy)

Strawberry Picking

Strawberry picking is a fun activity that allows you to connect with nature and enjoy the delicious taste of fresh strawberries. Grown all over the world, strawberries are often made the stars of festivals and classes on how to use what you harvest. Going to a berry farm is a great way to support local agriculture and communities while creating lasting memories with your family and friends. I have gone each year since my daughter was born, and we look forward to it each time. Can I just tell you, a fresh strawberry picked straight from the plant is beyond sweet, juicy, and quite literally the best strawberry you've ever tasted. Research and see if where you live has a local farm, and know that the season is usually short (around six weeks). Don't miss it!

Dyeing Eggs with Nature

This is a fun activity for the whole family! In spring, dyeing eggs with items you have on your homestead is a wonderful way to achieve beautiful natural color—and get egg-cited for the season. Here are the formulas I use.

NATURALLY DYED EGGS

YOU WILL NEED

Large stockpot

Ingredients for one color of your choice

Water to cover all of the ingredients being used

Fine-mesh strainer

Baking dish or another container

¼ cup (60 ml) white distilled vinegar

12 white or brown unpeeled hard-boiled eggs, at room temperature (Note: Do *not* use raw eggs.)

Paper towels

COLORANTS

4 cups (360 g) chopped purple cabbage produces blue on white eggs, green on brown eggs.

4 cups (4 g) red onion skins produces lavender on white eggs or red on brown eggs.

4 cups (4 g) yellow onion skins produces orange on white eggs, rusty red on brown eggs.

4 cups (900 g) shredded beets produces pink on white eggs, maroon on brown eggs.

½ cup (54 g) ground turmeric produces yellow on white eggs.

4 standard-size tea bags of pure hibiscus tea produces lavender on white eggs.

Continued

Instructions

In a large stockpot, place the ingredient for the color you want and add enough water to cover it by 1 inch (2.5 cm).

Bring this to a boil over high heat, then reduce the heat to medium-high. You want the water to stay lively without boiling over.

Boil for about 1 hour, stirring occasionally to make sure nothing sticks to the bottom.

Let everything cool to room temperature, then pour it through a strainer and into a deep baking dish. Discard the boiled material (you can compost it or feed it to your chickens, if you have them).

Add ¼ cup (60 ml) of vinegar to the dye.

Add the eggs to the dye, taking care not to crack them.

Leave the eggs in for at least 1 to 2 hours and up to 24 hours, because they will not darken right away. You can take some out at different times. I usually keep some in for 1 to 2 hours, some for 3 to 4, and some for the whole 24 hours.

As you remove each egg, pat it dry with a paper towel. The colors, especially the deep blues, will continue to develop.

NOTE: IF YOU WANT TO EAT THE EGGS THAT YOU DYED FOR JUST 1 OR 2 HOURS, MAKE SURE TO REFRIGERATE THEM IMMEDIATELY AFTER YOU REMOVE THEM FROM THE DYE. IT'S ALSO A GOOD IDEA TO REFRIGERATE THE OTHERS WHEN THEY ARE NOT BEING DISPLAYED, BECAUSE THEY ARE HARD-BOILED. IF YOU'VE LET THE EGGS SIT IN THE DYE FOR MORE THAN 2 HOURS, YOU PROBABLY SHOULDN'T EAT THEM, AS BACTERIA COULD HAVE STARTED TO DEVELOP. IF DISPLAYING THE EGGS, YOU CAN KEEP THEM IN THE REFRIGERATOR UNTIL IT'S TIME TO DISPLAY THEM.

Summer

I love summer, with its warm embrace of the sun and the days that stretch long into the night, accompanied by the splendor of starry skies. The air is filled with the sweet fragrance of freshly mowed grass, and blooming flowers add so much color to the outside. In the evening, the serenade of frogs and the flickering glow of fireflies cast a magical ambience. It's a time to create memories outdoors. At Azure Farm, the summer days are brimming with activity, from planting and harvesting in the flourishing garden to rotating the grazing animals around the pastures to give them respite from the sweltering heat. The beehives yield a sweet harvest of honey, and canning season springs to life. There's laundry swaying on the line, and I make lemonade all the time. What better way to spend a summer afternoon than with a summer picnic under an azure blue sky?

Outdoor Picnic

Having an outdoor picnic is a yearly tradition for me that I cannot miss. It's a wonderful opportunity to savor the yummy foods we've grown while spending quality time with loved ones. To start, try making some homemade bread (see page 192). For a mouthwatering topping, you can't beat fresh-from-the-garden bruschetta (see page 37).

Here are a few more tips to help make your picnic an unforgettable experience.

- Have your picnic somewhere you feel comfortable, even just in your backyard. It's the action of sitting on a blanket out in the open air that makes it fun. Find a large tree for shade, and it will give you a nice place to sit with a cool breeze.

- Get a special outdoor blanket for your picnic and use it every year.

- Bring some activities to do together. Flying a kite, playing a card game, reading books together, and playing ring toss are some of our favorites.

- Make a treat that you only enjoy on your special picnic day. This could be something seasonal, such as a dark chocolate mint truffle (see recipe at right) or homemade sun tea (see page 38).

GARDEN-FRESH BRUSCHETTA

Fresh tomatoes, preferably a meaty variety, homegrown

Salt

Fresh bread (see page 192)

Fresh basil, chopped, preferably homegrown

Balsamic glaze, optional

Instructions

The day before your picnic, chop the tomatoes to the size you want and then transfer them with as little liquid as possible to a bowl.

Sprinkle the tomatoes with a little salt, cover the bowl, and refrigerate it overnight.

Slice the bread into pieces ¼ inch (6 mm) thick. If you prefer it to be a little crispy, you can toast it lightly or slice it the night before and leave it out. (This won't work if the air in your house is humid.)

Before serving, drain the excess liquid from the tomatoes, add the chopped basil, and serve as a bread topping. Drizzle with balsamic glaze, if desired.

Some crunchy pickles (see page 156) and a refreshing homemade lemonade (see page 18) made with lavender simple syrup (see page 126) make delightful accompaniments.

DARK-CHOCOLATE MINT TRUFFLE

YOU WILL NEED

½ cup (120 ml) full-fat coconut milk

1½ teaspoons peppermint extract

1 cup (175 g) dark chocolate chips

½ cup (60 g) cocoa powder

Parchment paper

Instructions

In a small pot over medium heat, heat the coconut milk and peppermint extract together until steaming. Don't allow it to burn!

Add the chocolate chips and remove from the heat.

Stir until the chips melt completely.

Pour the mixture into a deep dish and freeze for 2 hours.

Using a spoon, scoop out enough to roll into a 1-inch (2.5 cm) ball. Repeat until you use all the truffle mix.

Roll the balls in cocoa powder and place them on parchment paper.

Refrigerate until serving. They'll keep for up to 5 days.

HOMEMADE SUN TEA

You've not truly experienced summer until you make sun tea. It's easy to do and a favorite family activity. The best moments we experience are when we slow down to enjoy all the goodness nature offers.

YOU WILL NEED

1 gallon (3.8 L) or quart (1 L) jar

Delicious water (filtered is good)

Fresh peppermint (½ cup [48 g] per quart [1 L], 2 cups [192 g] per gallon [3.8 L]) OR 6 tea bags per quart/10 per gallon

Sunshine (no electricity or energy required)

Raw honey, to taste

Instructions

Fill the jar with water, leaving room for the mint or tea bags.

Add the peppermint or the tea bags and seal tightly.

Place the jar in the sun and under the moon for 24 full hours. Because the mint is antifungal, it won't mold in this amount of time. The longer it sits, the darker the tea will be.

Strain out the herbs or remove the tea bags. Sweeten with honey as desired.

Keep refrigerated and enjoy.

NOTE: IF YOU ARE CONCERNED ABOUT THE TEA MOLDING OR BEING UNSAFE TO DRINK, YOU CAN SIMPLY BREW IT IN THE SUN FOR A MAXIMUM OF 4 HOURS AND STILL ENJOY THE DELICIOUS FLAVOR IT HAS TO OFFER.

Fall

Fall brings a burst of bright orange leaves and all things pumpkin. After the hot summer, the crisp autumn air feels refreshing. From apple picking to festivals, fall might bring some of the most fun traditions to do together as a family. As the sun sets earlier each day, there are also more opportunities to cook delicious meals together by the fire and enjoy each other's company.

Fall at Azure Farm keeps me busy. I plant various vegetables, such as beets, broccoli, and cabbage, to ensure a plentiful fall harvest. I begin the deep-litter method in the chicken coop to keep my birds warm as the days get cooler. A big delivery of hay comes in, and we stock up on feed. Inventory is taken of the pantry, and items are restocked as needed. My daughter helps me plant tulip bulbs; we all anticipate their colorful blooms come spring. As a family, we treasure the gifts that fall brings, and perhaps one of our favorite ways to experience those cozy nights is by a crackling campfire.

Campfire

I find a good campfire in the fall to be equivalent to a fun picnic in the summer. It warms the soul as much as it does your toes and fingers. You don't need a huge campfire; a small firepit will do. Just ensure you have a cooking grate to place over it if you want to make any food. Here are a few fun things to do by the campfire. (Always be sure to follow safe practices when making a fire and ensure it is in an approved area.)

- Make a pizza together! Use the pizza dough recipe found on page 194 and cook it in a cast-iron skillet over the fire. Use parchment paper for easy removal and cleanup. Have everyone add their favorite toppings, and enjoy! The key to making campfire pizza is to cook the crust first, flip it in the pan, then add your sauce and toppings.

- Bring a guitar if you have one, and sing together. The campfire is a great place for music.

- Make roasted-berry s'mores (see below). Seriously, it's a twist on the classic s'mores and so very good.

- Make popcorn over the campfire! So salty and good.

- Create your own outdoor movie theater by securing a white sheet onto the top and bottom of two wooden rods. Use an outdoor projector and relive the fun memories you've captured on family videos from the previous years and see how much everyone has grown.

ROASTED-BERRY S'MORES

This twist on the classic is so very good.

YOU WILL NEED

Frozen berries you put up over the summer (store-bought is okay, too)

Maple syrup

Pure vanilla extract

Cardamom

Instructions

Preheat the oven to 450°F (232°C).

Spread the frozen berries evenly on a rimmed baking sheet.

Drizzle the berries with a little maple syrup and a bit of vanilla, and sprinkle with a pinch of cardamom.

Roast until the berries are tender, about 25 minutes, then let them cool before you transfer them to a serving dish.

Make your s'mores as usual and top them with a drizzle of fruit sauce. It will be your new favorite!

NOTE: ENSURE YOU HAVE PERMISSION TO LIGHT A BONFIRE AND FOLLOW STANDARD FIRE SAFETY PROTOCOLS.

SALT DOUGH LEAF ORNAMENTS

Fall is a beautiful time to reflect on the year and be thankful for all the wonderful things accomplished thus far. Each year, I do a project with leaves, and these salt dough ornaments are great. I like to ask my daughter what she is thankful for each day. We write it on the leaf before we hang it. You can display the leaves around your home and even hang them from a branch to display. I have also tied them around a napkin as a unique napkin ring. They make a beautiful keepsake for years to come.

YOU WILL NEED

1 cup (120 g) all-purpose flour, plus more if needed

1 cup (240 g) salt

Up to 1 cup (240 g) warm water per color used

Food coloring (I chose green, red, and yellow)

Disposable gloves, optional

Pinch of nutmeg

2 tablespoons (12 g) ground cinnamon

Wax paper or other material to protect surfaces

Rolling pin

Leaf-shaped cookie cutters

Wooden skewer, toothpick, or sharp knife

Parchment paper

Baking sheet

Fine-tip permanent marker

Mod podge or ceramics glaze, optional

Twine, string, or yarn

Instructions

Mix the flour and salt in a bowl, then add warm water in small amounts, mixing as you go. It should come together as a slightly sticky dough. If it's sticky enough that residue comes off on your fingers, it means there is too much water. Add small amounts of flour until you get the right consistency.

Divide the mixture into three parts and add some food coloring to each dough ball. I recommend 4 or 5 drops, but you can add more if a darker color is desired. If you're a pro at making salt dough and already know the perfect balance of water and flour, add the food dye to the water before mixing it in. This will give the dough more even color throughout.

Wearing disposable gloves, if desired, work the dough with your hands, adding dye as necessary, until you're satisfied with the color.

Add the nutmeg and cinnamon. We added the cinnamon to all the dough balls but saved the nutmeg for the browner shade, which gave it most of its color.

On a sheet of wax paper or parchment paper, roll out the balls with a rolling pin to around ½ inch (1 cm) thick. With a leaf cookie cutter, cut out leaves, gathering the dough scraps and rerolling as necessary to cut as many leaves as possible. Using a toothpick or sharp knife, make a small hole at the top of each leaf to string through whatever you'll use to hang the leaf (twine, string, yarn, etc.).

Preheat the oven to 212°F to 284°F (100°C to 140°C).

Lay the finished creations on a parchment paper–lined baking tray and place in the oven for around 4 hours.

If the leaves are still doughy or soft after this time, turn them over and heat them again. The idea is to use the oven to air-dry and harden them, not to cook them.

Once the hardened leaves cool, use the permanent marker to write a word describing what you are thankful for on the back.

Seal each leaf with mod podge or glaze, if desired.

Tie a piece of twine, string, or yarn to the leaf and it is ready to hang on a tree, branch, or anywhere you see fit!

Winter

Shorter days call for more time indoors, making winter the perfect season for warm drinks and comfort food. Picture cozy mornings spent indulging in delectable baked pears right out of the oven (see page 174). There is a palpable sense of tranquility as nature rests under a blanket of snow. The crispness of winter air on my cheeks is a welcome feeling after summer's humid days. At Azure Farm, winter brings an opportunity to organize and clean up the greenhouse and garden spaces. Water heaters are strategically placed in the troughs to prevent freezing on cold nights. The farm itself is adorned with foraged wreaths and twinkling lights, adding to the ambience of winter. As late winter approaches, we trim fruit trees and order new seeds, ensuring a productive season ahead. While we do find time to rest, we also engage in play, recognizing the life-giving nature of spending time outside, especially when the days are shorter. Regardless of where you live, families can enjoy numerous activities together to embrace the outdoors and appreciate the beauty that winter brings.

Winter Scavenger Hunt

One of my daughter's favorite pastimes is foraging for treasures around the farm—so much so that we have a scavenger hunt every season. A winter scavenger hunt is an adventure full of seasonal charm. Invite friends and family to bundle up in cozy layers and get outside to explore. Each clue and hidden treasure becomes an exhilarating challenge to uncover amid the wintery scenery. After you're done exploring, you can treat everyone to some homemade pie (see page 190 for my flaky crust pie recipe).

Our scavenger hunts always include collecting or identifying natural elements around the farm. Here are some ideas:

- Acorns
- Animal tracks, such as from a dog or a bird
- Bare tree
- Bird nest
- Cardinal or other identifiable bird species
- Fallen leaves
- Feathers
- Flowers
- Ice
- Icicle
- Mushrooms
- Pine needles
- Pinecones
- Singing bird
- Snowflake
- Squirrel
- Winter berries

DIY FROZEN SUNCATCHER

On a cold winter's day, I look for ways to entertain Ava and spend some time outside. We can easily get caught up indoors when it's cold, rainy, and gloomy, so time outdoors has to be intentional and fun during the winter months. With the treasures we find on our scavenger hunt, we make a frozen suncatcher that glistens in the sunshine outside. It is so easy to make, completely free, and the kids love it—it's a win-win-win! Best of all, you can make a different one whenever the one you made melts. If you live somewhere super cold and it does not go above freezing, you can enjoy it for multiple days. You could also make a wildlife- and bird-friendly one by adding seeds for them to pick at. It's something fun to keep the birds busy!

YOU WILL NEED

Items foraged from nature (like the ones from your scavenger hunt, see page 45)

Sliced citrus, optional

Herbs, optional

Festive outdoor items, optional

Birdseed, optional

Pie pan

Water

String, yarn, or twine

Instructions

Select your outdoor treasures and place them in a pie pan or other shallow dish, making groupings of things that pair beautifully together.

Fill the pan to the brim with water.

Add a long piece of string, putting both ends in the water but leaving a long enough loop dangling outside so you can hang the suncatcher.

Place the pan in the freezer, keeping it flat. When frozen, carefully remove the suncatcher from the pan and hang it somewhere you can see it and enjoy it!

BRINGING NATURE INTO YOUR HOME

———

Since I can't always be outdoors, I love weaving nature into my daily life inside my home. Yes, it can be as simple as bringing in some flowers, but it runs deeper than that: opening the windows and allowing in the fresh air, growing fresh herbs near a window, decorating with items foraged from our backyard. These are all simple elements that can make your house a home and your home your absolute favorite place.

Decorating with Plants

I used to run to the nearest Target for the latest trends in home décor. Now, I run to the outdoors and let nature inspire me. It is honestly so much fun, especially when I do it with my daughter. Here are some ways we bring the outdoors in through decorating.

Branches

Branches are a quick way to add height and presence to any space. If the branch is flowering, that's a bonus. For me, the bigger the branch, the better. Spring is a favorite time to do this when there are delicate blooms on branches everywhere. But don't limit yourself to just one season. Fall branches with leaves in jewel tones are just as impressive. To decorate with branches, simply go outside to your yard. More than likely, you have a tree or two that could use a trim, and those fresh branches will do the trick. If not, you can forage from a friend's yard, perhaps—but always get permission before grabbing your pruners. I was outside a lovely antique shop one spring and it had the most gorgeous wisteria hanging right outside. I asked if I could grab some and the lady was quite excited about my appreciation of the beautiful lavender blooms. I brought my branch home and put it in a glass vase on my counter. For the next ten days, it brought me pure joy. Little things like that make me appreciate country living. There is no need for extravagance, just simple, natural details to make a home feel special.

Tips for Foraging Branches

Forsythia, magnolia, pear, pussy willow, and wisteria are some of my favorite flowering branches to bring inside. For long-lasting blooms, choose a branch with buds rather than open flowers. Here are some tips for bringing in any kind of branch.

- Check any branches for pests or dirt before you bring it into your house.
- When bringing branches indoors, set the ends in room temperature water.

- Choose a sturdy vase that will hold the weight of your branch so it does not send the vase tumbling. A heavy, pear-shaped container with a wide base is perfect.
- Keep the branch away from direct sun but in a room with lots of light.
- Recut the ends with a diagonal cut every day. This lets the branch keep taking up water and will help it last longer.
- Change the water daily.

Flowers

I will admit flowers are the easiest way to bring nature in—but I don't mean flowers you pick up at the store. What I'm talking about is the experience of finding ways to bring the beauty of the outdoors in. The satisfaction of, for example, gathering flowers from your own backyard, experiencing their beauty as they sway in the breeze, the scent that wafts through the air as you brush against the petals. Over the years, I've found it challenging to forage for the unique and unexpected. Each season brings new flowers to forage for and incorporate into my home.

Plant tulip, hyacinth, and daffodil bulbs in the fall for colorful blooms in the spring. Other beautiful spring flowers include lilacs, forsythias, and peonies. I have found daisies to be very easy to grow. A few years back, I tossed some on a hill near our home, and now they return each year. The crisp white flowers dance in the wind, bringing pure joy when picked and brought inside. Even better? Make a crown of daisies. It's the perfect family activity. Sunflowers are a must for summer and fall. Dahlias, zinnias, and cosmos bloom in my garden and are perfect as cut flowers. Check out chapter 4 for more on flowers and my favorite ones to grow. You can even have flowers indoors in winter with a Christmas cactus. Get creative, and don't be afraid to step out of the box when incorporating flowers into your home.

Foraged Items

Every season, I look to nature when I decorate. Foraged décor is beautiful and earthy, and it also does not cost you anything. Over the last few years, I have foraged for pine, cedar, and juniper, then added some dried hydrangea and magnolia leaves, pinecones, and holly to make wreaths each holiday. You can also add some culinary herbs, such as rosemary for a fresh scent.

In the fall, I love to use the pampas grass from our yard in a tall vase for a statement piece in the living room. They also look great as a floor display. Ferns, dry grasses, and seed pods bring beautiful texture and interest to your floral arrangements and home décor.

When foraging, the goal is to use what nature naturally gives us. Be mindful when gathering and respectful of the plants so you don't damage them. Do a little research on your area and climate before foraging. Familiarize yourself with plants that may be poisonous or endangered and always ask for permission if foraging on someone else's property

Herbs and Houseplants

I love keeping indoor plants. They bring instant cheer and color to my living spaces and offer some benefits too. Keeping plants in your home improves air quality by absorbing carbon dioxide and releasing oxygen. A few of my favorite indoor plants include snake plant (*Dracaena trifasciata*), pothos (*Epipremnum aureum*), fiddle-leaf fig (*Ficus lyrate*), and dwarf Meyer lemon tree (*Citrus limon* x 'Meyeri').

Growing herbs indoors is also a wonderful way to bring nature in. I love how easy it is to add color and flavor to meals with herbs. Choose a sunny spot near a window; use well-draining soil; and select herb varieties suited for indoor growth, such as basil, mint, or thyme. Water regularly and provide adequate airflow. Keep them pruned to encourage new growth and you'll have herbs year-round.

THE NATURAL HOME

As my love for the great outdoors blossomed, I couldn't help but feel a deep connection to nature. Growing my food and understanding the importance of what I consume was a vital part of my journey, and this trickled into wanting to make changes inside my home, as well. Everything changed when my daughter came into the world. Suddenly, I became acutely aware of the toxins around us daily. How could I breathe fresh air outdoors while still subjecting my home to toxin-containing products? That's when I shifted gears and gradually transformed our living environment by making my own products. This way, I'd know exactly what ingredients were in them. Plus, I discovered the joy of finding clever ways to reduce waste and repurpose items around my home.

Living a nature-inspired, healthy life has become my goal. Admittedly, the journey isn't a quick fix. It takes time and patience, but I embrace each step. And you know what? I truly believe that my family and I are healthier because of it. It's amazing how small changes can make a big difference in our well-being. Is my home "100 percent natural"? No. I still have room to grow. But I hope the following suggestions inspire you to make a few simple changes that will ultimately make a big difference.

Reducing Food Waste

Being the heart of the home, the kitchen is the first place I made some big changes. I admit I have tossed so much food, not knowing ways to reuse or repurpose it. There is no reason to waste food, but according to the United States Department of Agriculture, we waste 30 to 40 percent of our food supply. Finding alternative uses can be easy. Have an abundance of ripe produce? Consider freezing, canning, or pickling it using the methods in chapter 5 to prevent waste. Or make some crunchy veggie chips!

Composting is an easy way to literally reap the benefits of scraps (see chapter 3), but so much of what we throw away can be used to make other wholesome food, such as vegetable broth (see chapter 6), citrus seasoning, or Lemon Powder (see recipe opposite).

VEGETABLE CHIPS

YOU WILL NEED

Fresh, clean peels from root vegetables (potatoes, sweet potatoes, beets, and parsnips all work well)

Oil (neutral or flavored)

Salt, optional

Seasoning, optional

Baking sheet

Instructions

Preheat your oven to 400°F (204°C).

Rinse the peels and pat them dry. If they are wet, they'll steam instead of crisping.

Drizzle lightly with oil, sprinkle with salt and seasonings, as desired, and toss to coat. Spread on a baking sheet.

Bake for 20 to 25 minutes, flipping the chips halfway through the time. Remove when the chips are as crispy as you want them.

Let cool and enjoy!

LEMON POWDER

Use this easy-to-make powder in recipes that call for lemon zest or anywhere you want a bit of lemon flavor. Simply peel your lemons, including the pith, before using them for something else. You can keep the "naked" lemons in the fridge for up to a week or squeeze and freeze the lemon juice. Be sure to wash and rinse the lemons before peeling them.

YOU WILL NEED

Organic lemon peels

Baking sheet, preferably rimmed

Parchment paper

Coffee grinder* or high-powered blender

Airtight container

Instructions

Preheat your oven to 170°F (77°C).

Spread your peels on a baking sheet lined with parchment paper and place them in the oven for 2 to 3 hours, or until fully dry. The idea is to dehydrate the peels rather than bake them. Let them cool.

Blend the dried, cooled peels until fine in a clean coffee grinder or high-powered blender.

Store in an airtight container.

*IF YOU USE YOUR COFFEE GRINDER AS INTENDED—FOR COFFEE—BE SURE TO CLEAN IT VERY WELL BEFORE AND AFTER MAKING THIS RECIPE TO AVOID COFFEE-FLAVORED LEMON POWDER OR LEMON-FLAVORED COFFEE. ALTERNATIVELY, YOU CAN KEEP A COFFEE GRINDER ON HAND THAT YOU USE EXCLUSIVELY FOR SPICES AND SEASONINGS. YOU CAN MAKE THIS POWDER WITH LIME PEELS AS WELL.

The Role of Chickens

We repurpose some of our kitchen scraps by giving them to our chickens and in return we get fabulous compost and the best eggs in the world. Chickens are omnivorous and valuable in reducing food waste. These feathered friends efficiently convert kitchen scraps and leftovers into valuable nutrients. By feeding chickens vegetable peelings, fruit scraps, or stale bread, they enjoy a varied diet and turn scraps into nutrient-rich eggs and manure instead of landfill material. They are allies in the quest for a more sustainable and resourceful approach to food consumption.

I consider chickens to be the gateway animal into country living. They offer a simple and affordable entry point for those seeking a simple lifestyle. With minimal space requirements and basic care, raising chickens is a manageable endeavor, even for a beginner. Through tending to their needs, I gained invaluable animal husbandry knowledge and developed a deeper understanding of self-sustainability.

Chickens also have the remarkable ability to bring communities together. Whether it's sharing eggs or exchanging chicken-related knowledge, these fun birds create opportunities for social bonds and camaraderie. Witnessing the connections forged through a shared love for these animals is heartwarming. If you're looking for one animal that can benefit you and your home in multiple ways, think about adding chickens.

Natural Cleaning

Many store-bought household cleaners rely on harsh ingredients to get the job done. While some of these, such as bleach, are natural, others are synthetic. Once I discovered that gentler, homemade cleaners very often could be just as effective, without the chemical odors or label warnings, making the switch was easier.

Vinegar

At 5 percent acetic acid, vinegar can kill or reduce some kinds of fungi, viruses, and bacteria, including listeria, salmonella, and *E. coli*. All of the many kinds of vinegar are antimicrobial, but distilled white, sometimes called household, vinegar is the one most commonly associated with cleaning. Alone or combined with other ingredients (see Vinegar Combinations to Avoid on page 59 for exceptions), it also works against grime, rust, and soap scum. Equal parts water to vinegar works great as an all-purpose cleaning spray. Use it to clean your windows and glass panes, such as shower doors, and add 1½ to 2 cups (360 to 480 ml) to the bottom of your dishwasher, along with your usual detergent, to get shinier glasses and plates.

NOTE: AVOID GETTING VINEGAR OR A VINEGAR SOLUTION ONTO WOODEN OR METAL SURFACES.

Lemon

Delicious in beverages and food, this citrus fruit is also a potent cleaning tool. The acid in lemons is antibacterial and antiseptic and acts as a natural bleach. It can be used in many ways around the home.

- **Cutting Boards and Counters.** You can cut a lemon in half and dip it into salt as a scrubber for your cutting boards and countertops.
- **Toilet Bowl.** Squeeze half a lemon into the bowl, sprinkle a bit of salt, and give it all a good scrub with the toilet brush. Add baking soda or borax to the mix for even more stain-fighting power!
- **Faucets.** Rub half a lemon onto your chrome, brass, or copper faucets, then rinse. It will leave them squeaky clean.
- **Garbage Disposal.** This one is my favorite. Place half a lemon in your garbage disposal with a handful of ice and turn it on. It will clean it, sharpen the blades, and leave your kitchen smelling fresh.
- **Stained Clothes.** Treat clothing stains with a lemon juice and salt solution. Squeeze lemon juice directly onto the stain until it is covered. Add enough salt to cover the stain and let the mixture sit for 30 minutes. Rinse with vinegar and warm water. See the next section for more laundry tips.

VINEGAR-LEMON ALL-PURPOSE CLEANING SPRAY

I like to make this all-purpose cleaning spray for countertops, bathrooms, and even our chicken coop. Lemon oil has antibacterial and antifungal properties, making it a good cleaner and disinfectant.

YOU WILL NEED

1 cup (236 ml) distilled white vinegar

16-ounce (473 ml) spray bottle

25 drops lemon essential oil

1 cup (236 ml) water

Instructions

Pour the vinegar into the spray bottle and add the lemon oil.

Fill the remainder with water and you're ready to go!

Baking Soda

Baking soda has many benefits in the home and works wonderfully to absorb odors. It is also slightly abrasive, giving it good scrubbing power.

- Mix baking soda with water to form a paste, then use it to wipe down your oven and stovetop, eliminating grease in the process. Or use the paste to shine and remove spots from stainless steel, wiping it clean.

- An open box or a bowl of baking soda in the refrigerator can freshen foul smells.

- Sprinkle baking soda on bad-smelling upholstery, carpets, pet beds, and your mattress. Let it sit for 15 minutes, then vacuum it up.

- Unclog a drain by pouring ½ cup (118 g) of baking soda down, followed by ½ cup (120 ml) of vinegar. Wait 5 minutes and flush with hot water. Be careful of the fumes!

Castile Soap

This nontoxic, biodegradable soap is a green cleaning product that works wonders on almost anything. It is made from plant-based oils such as coconut, hemp, sunflower seed, jojoba, or, most commonly, olive. Here are a few ways you can use it around the home.

Vinegar Combinations to Avoid

Vinegar by itself or paired with other ingredients can make fast work of your cleaning chores, but combined with the wrong thing, it can be dangerous—even deadly! **NEVER** mix vinegar with any of these!

- Vinegar and Bleach
- Vinegar and Hydrogen Peroxide
- Vinegar and Baking Soda

- **All-Purpose Cleaning Spray.** Mix 6 cups (1.4 L) of water with ¼ cup (60 ml) of castile soap and 5 to 10 drops of your favorite essential oil for a big batch that should last you a while. It has a shelf life of about 6 months.

- **Floor Cleaner.** Add ¼ cup (60 ml) of castile soap to 2 gallons (7.6 L) of warm water and start scrubbing.

- **Liquid Hand Soap.** Mix 2 tablespoons (30 ml) of castile soap with 2½ cups (590 ml) of water and 10 to 12 drops of your favorite essential oil in a soap dispenser.

- **Produce Wash.** Use it to safely wash down your fruits and veggies.

The Natural Laundry Room

Your skin is your largest organ. Below are a few recipes and how-to's for everyday laundry use. Cleaning your clothes more naturally with gentler products prevents harmful toxins from getting into your skin. One simple way to experience the outdoors' benefits is to dry your clothes outside.

Line-Drying Laundry

Hanging laundry on a clothesline to dry offers numerous benefits. First, it is as energy-efficient and environmentally friendly as it gets. With no need for electricity or gas, it produces zero carbon emissions and lowers your monthly utility bill. I have also found it to be gentler on fabrics, preventing damage or shrinkage. I'm sure I'm not the only one who has shrunk clothing in the dryer.

Line-drying also provides a fresh scent without the need for artificial fragrances. You can hang fresh herbs along with your clothes to give them an even stronger scent. I recommend bunches of lavender, lemon thyme, and even roses. Sunlight aids in bleaching, disinfecting, and freshening fabrics, especially white and light-colored garments. Moreover, air-drying minimizes wrinkles, reducing the need for ironing or steaming. If you're anything like me, ironing clothes is not your favorite activity.

Hanging clothes on a line allows for a connection with nature, appreciating the outdoors, and taking a moment to slow down and enjoy the process. You don't need a fancy setup. I bought a simple kit online to hang clothes outside between two spaces. It's easy and something I encourage you to do if you've never tried it.

Inspiring Others through Nature

Inspiring others to enjoy nature can be a wonderful way to foster a deeper connection with the natural world. Consider gifting potted plants, bird feeders, nature-themed artwork, gardening tools, or other such items to encourage others to engage with nature in their own spaces. Encourage creativity with DIY nature-inspired crafts, such as pressed flower gifts (see page 124), handmade planters from recycled materials, and garden markers (see page 94). Organize group hikes, nature walks, nature-themed scavenger hunts, or invite friends over for bonfire night to immerse them in the beauty of the natural world. Have family and friends come over and harvest fresh produce from your garden and cook a meal together. By doing all this, you can inspire others to embrace the wonders found in nature, and we will all benefit together because of it.

DIY REUSABLE DRYER SHEETS

These are a much more natural and sustainable alternative to store-bought dryer sheets. This combination will help decrease static and leave your clothes with a light scent. If you're looking for a quicker alternative, you can always use a wool dryer ball instead when drying your clothes. The vinegar smell will dissipate when drying, and the essential oil will leave a faint aroma. Your clothes will not smell as amazing as when you use a normal dryer sheet, but these are much better for you.

YOU WILL NEED

1 cup (236 ml) distilled white vinegar

20 drops essential oil of choice (I like lavender)

(2) 8-ounce (236 ml) jars with snug lids, such as canning jars

(10) 7 × 7-inch (18 × 18 cm) squares of cotton or flannel

Instructions

Add the vinegar and essential oil to a jar.

Soak your cotton squares in the mixture, then squeeze excess liquid back into the jar. Seal and store the jar if there is any leftover vinegar mixture.

Fold the squares and store them in another jar with a lid (they will remain damp in the jar until ready to use).

Add 1 or 2 to your load before running the dryer.

When you remove your dry clothes, re-wet the squares and place them back in your jar for later use.

NOTE: ESSENTIAL OILS ARE FLAMMABLE. BE SURE TO DILUTE IT IN THE VINEGAR AND ONLY ADD THE SPECIFIED AMOUNT.

DIY LAUNDRY DETERGENT

Spending so much time outdoors and running Azure Farm, our clothes can get very dirty. The ingredients in this recipe are the best combination I've found for getting them clean again, and I love the light scent of lemon it leaves. You'll be surprised at how inexpensive this is compared to store-bought detergent. It only costs me about five dollars to make a gallon (3.7 L) that lasts 30 to 40 loads!

YOU WILL NEED

14 cups (3.3 L) water (filtered, if you have hard water)

½ cup (118 g) salt

1 cup (120 g) baking soda

1-gallon (3.8 L) container with lid
(I use a glass jar)

Funnel, optional

1 cup (246 ml) lemon-scented castile soap or other soap, scented or unscented

30 drops lemon or other essential oil

Instructions

In a large pot, heat the water to boiling.

Stir in the salt and baking soda until it dissolves. Remove from the heat.

Pour the hot solution into a gallon container. A funnel can help.

Add the soap and the essential oil.

Use ½ to 1 cup (118 to 236 ml) per load. The mixture will solidify a bit between uses. Simply mix before pouring.

NOTE: I USE THIS WITH MY HIGH-EFFICIENCY TOP-LOADING WASHER, WHICH WORKS WELL. I HAVE READ A LOT ABOUT FRONT-LOADING WASHERS, AND IT SHOULD WORK WITH THESE, TOO. IT'S A LOW-SUDS FORMULA, SO IT SHOULDN'T BE AN ISSUE, BUT TRY YOUR FIRST LOAD CAREFULLY. THIS RECIPE DOES NOT WORK WELL WITH HARD WATER, SO USE FILTERED WATER IF THAT'S AN ISSUE.

CULTIVATING *a* GARDEN

J ust like deciding on a change of lifestyle, I had to find my gardening "why." Why did I want a garden? What was my motive for planting all those seeds?

I believe a life well lived starts with a garden. Since the dawn of time, humans have connected with the soil and plants. It is in our nature to crave the outdoors and sunshine on our faces. Sadly, modern conveniences have shifted our focus away from the living world around us and toward screens. For me, gardening is empowering. It lets me know where my food comes from, supplies me with food stability, and helps me provide for my family. It's a place for reflection, where I can witness the miracle of seeds sprouting into life and reap mental, physical, and spiritual benefits.

Of all the ways to live a simple life, gardening is the most significant. You can garden no matter where you live, and it doesn't have to be complicated. Some of my best results have come from just throwing seeds in the ground and watching them grow. Yes, there is typically more to it, but it does not have to be overwhelming or burdensome. Once you learn and apply some of the essentials to keeping a healthy garden, you'll soon gather all that life-giving harvest from your own backyard.

Gardening allows you to connect with nature in a more personal way. It's not just about growing plants. It's about cultivating a sense of purpose and appreciation for the world around you. I hope you find the same joy in getting your hands in the soil, cultivating, and harvesting.

ESSENTIALS TO A HEALTHY GARDEN

———

A healthy garden is a beautiful, productive space where plants can thrive. It benefits people and the environment. Successfully caring for a garden requires proper soil preparation, adequate water, and sunlight. I choose plants well suited to my climate and soil conditions, and I try to rotate crops and use companion planting to maintain soil health naturally. I love using organic methods instead of chemicals to control pests and diseases. Let me go a bit more in-depth on how I help our garden thrive.

Healthy Soil

The most important thing for you to remember from this chapter is this: Soil health is everything when it comes to successful gardening.

There is a difference between dirt and soil. We often use the two words interchangeably, but when it comes down to science, they have two meanings. Soil feeds and supports healthy plants; dirt does not. Dirt is what my daughter uses to make mud pies and kicks around her feet while playing. There's dust, grime, mud, and maybe even some pollutants in it.

Soil is what happens when natural matter decomposes into a dynamic ecosystem comprising minerals, organic materials, gases, water, and living organisms, most of which are microscopic. Why does that matter? Having healthy, nutrient-dense soil gives your plants what they need to provide you in turn with the most amazing, life-giving food.

Farming practices today are not the same as they were 100 years ago. We now grow the same crops in the same soil year after year. The ground is overworked and the soil is loaded with synthetic fertilizers to help make up the nutrient deficit. There are simple ways to keep your soil, and the surrounding land and water, healthy. Properly maintained soil is nutritious soil (for plants!), and healthy plants pass those nutrients on in the food they produce. Your soil will be healthy with the right minerals, compost, and organic matter.

One way to know your soil is healthy is by what's living in it. Yes, those earthworms and creepy-crawlies might be a bit intimidating to see or touch at first, but I promise you they are a big part of what makes your soil the perfect ecosystem for your plants.

If you want to start gardening and have no idea what condition your soil is in, begin with a soil test. This can help you analyze your soil's nutrient content, pH level (how acidic it is), and other properties to determine deficiencies. You can obtain soil test kits from many places, including local extension offices, garden centers, or nurseries, and even online. Once you determine your soil needs, it will be easier to amend from there.

Keep soil health at the forefront of all you do when starting a garden. I promise your results will be much better and you will receive the best health benefits, as well. There are health benefits to just sticking your hands in the soil each day. So take those gloves off and start planting. Please remember that your soil will not improve overnight. It takes time. It's trial and error and learning a little day by day. Stay the course, do what you can, and you will see the fruits of your labor in time.

Natural Soil Amendments

We use a few different ways to amend soil on Azure Farm.

- Well-rotted leaves. I have used leaves for years in our garden beds. They break down into rich organic matter that helps the soil retain moisture and prevents erosion.

- Compost. My compost comes mainly from animal manure, but I also compost kitchen scraps. You'll find a whole section on composting later in this chapter.

- Mulch. Ideal for helping with water retention and weed suppression, mulch can include straw, grass clippings, or even wood chips. Here at the farm, I use a seedless straw that effectively suppresses weeds.

- Cover crops. If your soil is deficient in nutrients, consider planting a cover crop, such as clover or rye. Many are high in nitrogen and help feed the soil. Plant them and allow them to grow. Just before they go to seed, cut them back and till them in. As they decompose, they will give nutrients right back to your soil. A favorite of mine we plant in our garden beds in the fall is red clover.

Water, Drainage, and Sunlight

When starting a garden, remember the critical roles played by water, drainage, and sunlight.

We all know that plants need water to survive. The right amount is crucial for their health and growth. Overwatering can deprive the roots of oxygen and lead to disease. Insufficient watering will dry out the plants and lead to wilting. This has happened to me way too many times.

Even if you use the right amount of water, you need to be sure your plants have proper drainage. If the water doesn't drain well, you'll have the same issues as overwatering. If it drains too quickly, the plants won't have time to absorb it and will be less able to thrive, especially on a hot, sunny day.

Plants convert sunlight to energy. Each plant has different requirements, but most food plants need at least 6 hours per day of full sun to thrive. Not enough sunshine leads to stunted growth, poor flowering, and thus lower production. I discuss this in further detail on page 78.

Compost

Compost is a fantastic way to amend and add life to your soil. It is a mixture of organic materials, such as garden debris and food scraps, that decompose to make a soil-like mixture rich in nutrients and beneficial organisms. In simple terms, it is decaying natural matter. Why is it important?

Apart from being full of nutrients like phosphorus, nitrogen, and potassium, which are the three most important for plant growth, compost also helps improve soil structure by increasing its ability to retain water. It promotes biodiversity in your garden ecosystem by providing an ideal habitat for beneficial microorganisms, reducing the need for chemical fertilizers. Store-bought compost can be expensive, so making your own is a great alternative. You also reduce your waste footprint by tossing your veggie and fruit scraps into your compost! At first, I found the whole concept overwhelming, but it does not have to be.

To make organic matter compost, you need organic material: grass clippings, leaves, wood chips, fruits, vegetables, clean eggshells, and animal manure. Avoid meat, dairy, dead plants, oil, lard, or grease. When composting, think of adding green and brown materials, which will give a balance between high-nitrogen items and high-carbon components. If you have farm animals and want to compost their manure, I suggest doing two different compost areas— one for animal manure and one for your other organic matter.

Make a Compost Bin

There is no magical amount of time for creating compost. It can take a few months to even a year. Lemon peels, for example, can take a long time to decompose, which is why I recommend using citrus peels for other uses (see page 55). You'll know it's ready when it is a rich brown color, smells like the earth, and crumbles in your hand. It's not ready when food content is still visible, or the pile is hot to the touch. This means things are still breaking down.

Decide where to place your compost bin or area. You can easily create the space from pallets, wood boards, cinder blocks, or other materials. Our main bin is three-sided so I can put the matter in it through the front. Each of my compost areas is a different size and shape. If you're new to composting, I recommend starting small (3 × 3 feet [1 × 1 m]) so everything sits closely together and breaks down more quickly. Do what works best for you.

Add your natural materials. The smaller the material you add to the pile, the quicker it will break down. Turn it occasionally with a shovel to help aid in the breakdown. The more you turn it, the faster it will break down. This will also aerate your pile. Water can also help things break down, so if you live in a dry climate, water the pile occasionally and turn it to help accelerate the process.

Manure Compost

Animal manure is an excellent source of compost when used appropriately. Most fresh manure is so high in nitrogen that it will kill plants immediately. Manure from poultry, goats, cows, sheep, donkeys, pigs, and horses must be composted. Just follow the process outlined on page 70—preferably in a separate compost area.

There are, however, some animals whose manure is not as high in nitrogen and can be used immediately in the garden. Alpacas and rabbits are my favorites for this. Rabbit manure has four times the nutrients of cow or horse manure and is twice as rich as chicken manure. I've known people who live in an apartment in a big city with a pet rabbit. They use the droppings to add nutrients to their balcony garden.

We brought alpacas to Azure Farm specifically for their manure-producing abilities. They are not just cute; they mow our pasture—without uprooting the grass like sheep would—and provide our garden with the most amazing manure we use as fertilizer. To make it even better, alpacas use communal piles, so you can find their manure in an all-in-one spot without scooping it up from everywhere. That's not all. We shear our alpacas once a year, causing them no harm. Alpacas produce fiber, just as sheep produce wool. (Unlike sheep, alpacas are not raised for their meat.) While the fiber makes sought-after sweaters, blankets, and more, it also works as a moisture-retaining mulch. Mixing it directly into the soil improves the soil structure and prevents erosion.

No matter how you compost, know it is essential to healthy soil and your garden. There are no limits to how you can learn to do things more self-sustainably.

GARDEN PLANNING AND LAYOUT

———

One of my favorite yearly activities is planning a garden. I typically begin during the cold winter months when gardening isn't a daily task. It's exciting to imagine new plants and flowers to plant. However, before I started my first garden, I had to observe the land to determine the best location. This involved studying the sun's patterns to identify the area with the most sunlight, recognizing spots where water would accumulate during a rainstorm, and understanding local weather patterns that would impact my growing season. By familiarizing myself with these factors, I have had success year after year, and you can too.

Know Your Zone

I had no clue what a growing zone was when I started gardening. But knowing your growing zone is one of the easiest ways to ensure your garden will be successful. Sadly, not all plants grow in all places. Depending on where you live, some plants just won't do well due to too much heat or cold. I've often told my friends who live in California that I am pretty envious (in a good way) of their ability to grow lemons and avocados right in their backyards. Those trees would not survive our cold winters.

Around the world, every country has their zone, so it's an easy thing to look up. For the United States, they're called the USDA hardiness zones, and each zone has an assigned number. Northwest Georgia, where I live, is zone 7b, which means our average lowest temperature is between 5°F and 10°F (-15°C and -12°C). Once you know your hardiness zone, you can determine whether the plants you want to grow will work well in your area and when to start seeds indoors. Knowing your zone is one of the keys to having a successful garden.

Find Your Style

For many years, I didn't believe I could garden without a lot of space, fancy equipment, and the perfect setup. But the idea of having a large garden kept me from getting my hands in the soil and planting wherever and however I could. Now I understand that gardening doesn't have to be limited to a particular structure or space. With creativity and vision, you can turn even a tiny space into a garden oasis to grow your food and flowers. There are no rules when it comes to what you can plant in your garden, and it's a beautiful way to express your creativity. Not every type of garden may be right for you, but I believe gardening aims to connect us with the earth and provide a way to grow healthy food while improving our mood.

Gardening brings me pure joy, no matter where I plant my crops. Each year, my garden looks different as I add new plants or remove things that didn't work for me. I've succeeded in doing a little bit of everything and inviting nature into my garden space by creating a habitat for plants and beneficial insects to thrive. To determine what's best for you, consider your space, budget, and gardening goals.

Container Gardening

As a gardener, I find container gardening is an excellent choice for several reasons. First, it is a versatile option for those with limited outdoor space, such as an apartment. Containers can be placed on balconies, patios, and windowsills, allowing you to enjoy the benefits of gardening even in small spaces. Additionally, container gardening provides greater control over soil quality, drainage, and pest control. You can choose the specific soil mixture that suits your plants and water them more easily, ensuring their optimal health. Another advantage of container gardening is that you can move your plants around to take advantage of better sunlight, shade, and protection from extreme weather conditions. If you're new to container gardening, I recommend mixing a variety of plants together to get maximum results in a small space. For instance, planting parsley and basil in the same container can be an excellent choice. Cucumbers and herbs can also be a fun mixture, with cucumbers growing vertically on a trellis while herbs like oregano and dill thrive around the edges of the container. I've found that some herbs like mint, oregano, and thyme can take over a garden bed entirely if left alone. Growing them in containers—even if it's not your primary gardening method—keeps them under control while adding visual interest, beauty, dimension, and aroma to your garden space.

Raised-Bed Gardening

Raised bed gardening is a popular form of gardening where the planting bed sits on top of the existing soil and is raised from the ground. While it can be just a mound of soil, they are more typically enclosed in a frame made of lumber, stone, bricks, cinder blocks, or concrete. Raised beds can be as low as 6 to 12 inches (15 to 30 cm) off the ground or as tall as 30 inches (76 cm) or more. They work great when you have a very wet climate, compact or poor-quality soil, or are physically unable to garden low to the ground.

As with container gardening, one advantage of raised beds is that you have better control over the growing conditions, such as fertilizer, mulch, watering, and, most importantly, the soil. Native soil may be clay, silt, rocky, and contaminated with pesticides and weeds. Using raised beds filled with healthy soil and compost can ensure that your plants have optimal growing conditions. The roots of your plants will have ample space to grow, ensuring healthier, bigger plants. Raised beds also make it easier for you to notice and contain weeds. In fact, you can consider adding a weed barrier at the bottom when designing your raised beds. Additionally, raised beds warm up quicker than in-ground soil in the spring, allowing for a longer growing season, so you can get planting earlier.

SIMPLE RAISED BED FRAME

This easy project uses three 8-foot (2.5 m) boards, some hardware, and a few tools. Attach the boards for the short sides of the frame to the inside of the long sides to form a sturdy rectangle. Cedar is ideal here, as it naturally withstands elements and insects. If that's unavailable or too expensive, untreated pine will work. It should last about five years before it needs replacing, longer in a drier climate. I like to use a water-soluble stain on the outside of our beds to help them withstand the elements longer.

YOU WILL NEED

(3) 8-foot (2.5 m) cedar or untreated pine boards of your desired width

Sawhorses, optional

Measuring tape

Table saw or handsaw

C-clamps, optional

4 corner braces

Pencil

Power drill

Drill bits

Galvanized wood screws

Screwdriver, optional

Instructions

Saw one board into two equal lengths.

Working with the boards on their edges rather than flat, butt one cut board against one long board at one end to form an L. The long board's end should be visible, the cut board's end should be against the long board. Mark the cut board's placement.

Clamp or hold a brace in the corner formed by the two boards. Outline it and mark where to place the screws.

Drill starter holes in both boards for the screws.

Repeat for the remaining boards.

Screw the braces to the boards to assemble the frame.

If you build a tall raised bed, it will take a lot of soil to fill it. Consider adding some natural materials such as branches, leaves, and even a few rocks to help mimic the natural layout of the earth and give you organic matter that can decompose over time. Then you can add soil and compost on top of that organic matter. You'll fill that bed in no time.

While there are many advantages to raised beds, there are also some disadvantages. Raised beds are more expensive and are more permanent structures than planting directly in the ground. Also, not all crops do well in raised beds. For instance, watermelons and pumpkins need a lot of space to thrive, which is a bit harder with a raised bed.

In-Ground Gardening

This traditional way of gardening involves forming a distinct garden area within the ground by tilling, amending, and adding to the current soil. It may work better than raised beds in hot and dry climates or when your current soil structure and quality are optimal, and without the need to purchase building materials, it's also likely to cost less. Finally, you also have the option of a larger planting area and are not restricted to certain shapes or sizes.

Since in-ground gardening is not a permanent structure, you can change and rearrange things easily. In-ground gardening tends to dry out less quickly than raised beds, which means fewer irrigation requirements. Moreover, in-ground gardening allows for deep root growth, which can be beneficial for certain crops that require more space to grow, like pumpkins and watermelons. If you want to grow a variety of plants in a large area with few additional costs, then in-ground gardening might be the best for you.

The Ideal Garden Placement

To ensure that your veggies thrive and grow, they need full sun for at least 6 hours each day, so pay attention to your site's exposure when deciding on garden placement and layout. South-facing is ideal. If possible, take a few seasons to observe the space you want to use. Take note of how the wind moves and where the rain falls. Strong winds can impact plant growth, so consider what shelter your garden might need. In very hot climates, providing shade during the hottest part of the day may be necessary. One option is to place your garden facing east, which provides morning sun and some afternoon shade. Ultimately, the best direction for your garden will depend on various factors, and you will need to determine what works best for your growing space.

My Earliest Gardening Memories

When I was a child growing up in Texas, my dad was always growing something in our backyard. I vividly remember going outside to pick large heads of broccoli. A few years later, we moved to live in Kansas City, where my dad once again had a garden; he even planted fruit trees. We were in a neighborhood with houses visible on all sides, yet our small backyard was bursting with fresh produce: tomatoes and peppers, vines heavy with grapes, and pears from the trees. Seeing how much you could do in a small space made such an impression on me! Don't be limited by lack of space. No matter where you live, gardening is always possible if you use your imagination and discover the methods that best suit your lifestyle.

Design Something You Will Love

The garden is a place for the family to grow closer together. It's a place where many memories will be made. When creating a garden, it's not always feasible to achieve a flawless, magazine-like design. However, it's important to create a space that can be your own personal oasis. The garden is an extension of my home and I adore strolling through it and having a place to unwind. As you plan, think about who will be using the garden space. If you have little ones, create a designated spot for them to dig and play. This will inspire a love for growing things from a young age. My three-year-old daughter enjoys planting vegetables and flowers in her own garden bed. My goal has always been to instill in my family a love for nature. It's never too early—or too late—to start.

To get the most out of your garden, it's critical to create something that serves both aesthetic and functional purposes. Incorporate practicality and beauty into your design. For example, trellises are a great way to add vertical gardening space and visual interest. Flowers are an easy way to add beauty to a garden and also food for pollinators. When considering the width of pathways, think about whether a wheelbarrow will fit through your rows of plants. If your raised beds are too wide—I recommend keeping them no wider than 4 feet (1.2 m)—it may be difficult to reach the plants in the center.

Add pots, wind chimes, benches, and bird baths. Make it your own and you will want to spend time in your garden day after day.

CHOOSING SEEDS

There are so many kinds of seeds out there: heirloom, hybrid, genetically modified, organic or not, and more. I never used to pay much attention; I would just buy whatever caught my eye. There wasn't anything necessarily wrong with that, but in doing so, I limited myself to what my garden could be. In trying to follow a more natural lifestyle, we plant mostly organic and heirloom seeds. This way we know exactly what kind of plant we are growing and we can save those seeds for future use. Yes, I still buy some seedlings from the local nursery and grab random seeds that seem to call out to me when I walk by them at the hardware store, but for the most part, I try to use high-quality heirloom seeds. Here is the breakdown on seeds and what you need to know before you start planting.

Types of Seeds

Heirloom Seeds. These are seeds that have often been passed down for generations and are typically from varieties over fifty years old. They are open-pollinated, which means they are pollinated naturally by insects, bees, or the wind. The plants that grow from these seeds will be the same as their parent plants. They are a bit more unpredictable when it comes to yield, size, and so on, but their flavor, to me, is unmatched.

Hybrid or F1 Seeds. These seeds are usually created by deliberately crossing two different varieties of a plant to produce a new variety with characteristics of both. They are typically bred to resist disease and to produce larger crops and uniform fruit. Hybrids are not genetically modified organisms (GMOs). Hybrid seeds will not produce the same plant as the original. You can find organic hybrid seeds, which are what I would recommend planting if you are new to gardening and want to grow plants that will be resilient and disease resistant.

GMO seeds. These seeds have been genetically engineered to produce specific traits, such as resistance to pests or herbicides. Corn is one of the main veggies grown from genetically modified seeds. You cannot grow GMO seeds as a home gardener, as they are only reserved for commercial growers.

Organic Seeds. These seeds are the product of plants raised without the use of synthetic fertilizers or chemicals. They are often open-pollinated/heirloom varieties but can also be hybrids. There are a lot of heirloom seeds that are organic as well.

Benefits of Heirloom Seeds

There are several reasons why we choose to grow mostly heirloom seeds in our garden.

For starters, many heirloom seeds have interesting histories and stories behind them. Some super unique varieties like the 'Arkansas Traveler' tomato have been treasured and passed on for decades. By passing seeds on to the next generation, I can help preserve that history and promote sustainability.

Heirloom seeds are also unique because they are evergreen. I know every time I plant a yellow Brandywine tomato seed (my absolute favorite tomato variety), I will get to experience the same flavor from years before. Since heirlooms are passed down through generations, there are so many amazing varieties of veggies. Why grow orange carrots when you can have purple and white ones? Better yet, a blueish-purple radish! You could never get bored, and just think of all the amazing nutrients you put in your body when you eat all the colors of the rainbow.

It's crucial for me to know the seed has not been modified or engineered in some lab. With heirloom varieties, I do not need to buy new seeds every year but rather harvest seeds from this year's plant to use next year. I am not dependent on other businesses, the economy, or the food supply chain.

Lastly, the flavor is by far the best when it comes from heirloom produce. My husband always jokes that you don't even need to add salt to those delicious heirloom tomatoes. They have so much flavor. When comparing them to store-bought tomatoes, no one will say that homegrown isn't better by far.

NOTE: MY FAVORITE PLACE TO ORDER HEIRLOOM SEEDS IS BAKER CREEK SEEDS.

JARED'S SEED-STARTING SOIL MIX

My husband Jared developed this recipe with an old farmer years ago. It has a very high "brix" ratio, which means all of the ingredients work optimally together to create the perfect soil mixture, leading to higher germination and higher disease resistance.

YOU WILL NEED

6 quarts (5.7 L) coconut coir or peat moss

18 quarts (17 L) worm compost

½ quart (473 ml) gypsum

¼ quart (473 ml) molasses

2 quarts (1.9 L) alfalfa

¼ quart (236 ml) kelp

½ quart (473 ml) biochar

Instructions

Mix all ingredients together in a wheelbarrow.

Use this mixture when starting your seedlings.

When you're ready to transplant your seedlings, add a little bit of soil mix to each hole and then transplant.

NOTE: THERE IS ENOUGH IN THIS RECIPE TO FILL THREE 5-GALLON (19 L) BUCKETS. IT IS MY GO-TO WHEN PLANTING AND STARTING SEEDS. YOU CAN FIND MOST OF THESE INGREDIENTS ONLINE.

Understanding a Seed Packet

Although a seed packet can sometimes be overwhelming to read, it contains crucial information. A typical seed packet includes instructions on when and how to plant the seeds, including the recommended planting depth and spacing requirements. It should also note whether you can start the seedlings indoors or if you should direct sow them. If the packet indicates direct sow, you don't need to start the seeds indoors; you can plant them directly in the ground once the fear of frost has passed.

Additionally, the packet will inform you how many days it takes the seeds to sprout after planting. To keep track, it's helpful to note this on a calendar. For instance, the Chicago Pickling cucumber variety (think crunchy pickles) sprouts in 10 to 14 days. By marking the calendar on the planting date, you know when to expect little sprouts to pop up.

Following the directions on the seed packet provides the best chance for successful germination, which is the transition from seed to seedling. Store the seeds as recommended on the packet to keep them viable for the maximum amount of time.

SEED-STARTING BASICS

There really is magic in starting seeds. It does not matter how many times I have done it; every single time, I am *so* excited to see those little sprouts break through the soil. Just the other day, I literally did a little happy dance in my greenhouse when I saw sprouts from seeds I had planted five days prior. Seed starting does not have to be hard or use a lot of equipment. If you provide the seed with good soil, water, warmth, and sunlight, it will grow.

Starting my own seeds allows me to get a jump start on the growing season. It might be cold outside, but my little seedlings thrive indoors under controlled conditions and will be ready to plant as soon as the weather warms.

Before You Start

Since certain plant species and varieties are better adapted to specific climates and growing conditions, know your zone to ensure the seeds you choose are well suited for your climate. Do a quick internet search for your estimated first and last frost dates. If you want in-depth information on your city and surrounding area, I suggest talking with your local nursery. They are usually happy to help and educate on the subject. Write your frost dates down on your calendar. Now, look at your seed packet, which will tell you how many weeks before your last frost date to start your seeds. For example, it's best to start most tomatoes indoors 6 to 8 weeks before the average last frost date, which for me in zone 7b is usually April 15. Therefore, I start my seeds around the first week of March. Familiarize yourself with these terms and dates and it will help your gardening experience be a success.

Seed-Starting Supplies

Decide where you will start your seeds. Will you be doing it indoors near a window, in a room with a grow light, or possibly in a greenhouse? Depending on which, you might need fewer or more supplies.

I started my first seeds by a sunny window in our spare bedroom. I placed my seed trays on a table and had great success. Nothing fancy, yet it was effective. If you don't think you have a sunny and warm enough spot, place your seedlings under grow lights. These mimic the light of the sun and give your plants the light and boost they need to sprout and grow until they are ready to go outside. No matter where you start your seeds, you'll need the following:

- Compost
- Humidity dome (a lid for the tray)
- Labels
- Markers
- Plastic trays to go under your seed trays
- Seed-starting mix (I prefer organic)
- Seed trays
- Seeds

Most local gardening stores sell seed-starting kits that contain all these supplies, minus your seeds. I suggest getting trays that are on the larger side and made of sturdy plastic. Yes, plastic is not always the ideal choice, but take care of them and you can reuse those trays for years to come. Optional items, such as a seedling heat mat, might be nice if your plants will be started in a cooler place and need extra warmth, but they are not imperative. If you are starting your seeds inside your home, you won't need a seedling mat. I start my seeds in a greenhouse that stays warm but sometimes not warm enough. For that reason, I do use one from time to time. Keep in mind that most seedlings need a temperature of 60°F to 80°F (16°C to 27°C) to sprout. This is especially true for tomatoes and peppers. You can research the seeds you're growing to learn their specific preferences.

When choosing a seed-starting mix, I prefer to use one that is made of organic ingredients. Most seed-starting mixes, however, are just a combination of peat moss, vermiculite, and coconut coir, which provide a loose soil-type consistency for seeds but not a lot of nutrients. I have started seeds in this before and have not seen as much success as when I added some compost. So mix a little bit of worm castings, mushrooms, or cow manure compost with your seed-starting mix for the most success.

You can also use the seed-starting mix on page 82.

STARTING SEEDS

Organic seed-starting mix

Compost

Bucket or other container

Water

Seed-starting trays or small pots

Pen dibber or wooden skewer, optional (see Note)

Seeds

Plant labels

Pen or marker

Humidity dome

Instructions

Combine your seed-starting mix and compost in a bucket and add enough water to make it uniformly moist but not dripping. Squeeze out excess moisture, if necessary (see image 1).

Fill each tray cell or small pot with the mix.

Make a hole with a pen dibber, your finger, or a wooden skewer to the depth your seed packet indicates. A rule of thumb is to plant a seed twice as deep as the size of the seed, but some seeds need to be sown on the surface (see image 2).

Drop two or three seeds in each tiny cell. If you spill some, thin them out after they sprout (see image 3).

Water gently. Be careful not to waterlog the cells or wash out the seeds (see image 4).

Add a label and date. This is important! Unless you're only growing one kind of plant, I guarantee you will lose track of what you planted where.

Cover the seeds with the humidity dome and put them in a warm place until they sprout.

1)

2)

3)

4)

NOTE: A DIBBER IS A TOOL SPECIFICALLY FOR MAKING HOLES FOR SEEDS.

Hardening Off and Transplanting

Hardening off your plants involves taking them outside for short periods to help them adjust to their new surroundings. This step is particularly crucial if you start your seedlings indoors under grow lights, where they aren't exposed to direct sunlight and natural elements. Most plants require some degree of hardening off before planting. Take your seedlings outside for a couple of hours in the morning or evening, when the sun is less intense. Gradually increase the time they spend outdoors each day. Set a timer to ensure you don't forget to bring them back inside!

After 7 to 10 days, your seedlings should be fully acclimated and ready for transplanting. If you grow your seedlings in a greenhouse, you might be able to reduce the hardening-off time by half, provided they are already used to receiving the sun's rays throughout the day.

When it's time to transplant, do so in the early morning or evening to minimize shock to your seedlings. Add compost and fertilizer to the soil before planting to give your seedlings an extra boost, and water the soil well. Don't be alarmed if your plants initially look weak—they will likely bounce back after a day or two in their new home. Transplant day is exciting because in no time, you will see the fruits of your labor come to fruition!

CROP ROTATION

Crop rotation is an important practice that offers numerous benefits to your garden. It involves planting different crops in the same area over various seasons. This sustainable farming practice can enhance soil fertility, control pests and diseases, and reduce the need for fertilizers because it gives the soil a chance to recover the nutrients that the previous crop may have depleted. For example, leafy plants such as salad greens and Brassicas consume nitrogen in the soil; fruits such as tomatoes and peppers eat phosphorus; root veggies such as carrots and beets consume potassium. But legumes, such as peas and beans, restore nutrients to the soil.

Rotating your crops in a sequence is essential to replenish the soil season after season. This approach allows the soil to recover its nutrients and stay productive. Furthermore, if a particular plant has a disease in the soil, not planting the same variety in that location will reduce the risk of the disease recurring the following year. For instance, if you get squash bugs, they'll be less likely to infest your squash the following season if you plant them in a new location.

For the best results, only grow a particular vegetable or vegetable family in a particular location once every three or four years. For example, plant tomatoes in year one; carrots, beets, and similar root crops in year two; peas or beans in year three; and return to tomatoes in year four.

Now, you must give soil time to rest and replenish itself to expect it to produce a high yield. So, at times, it's essential to allow the soil to rest completely for some years and not plant anything in it at all. This is especially true if you reuse a space over and over. The Jewish nation historically followed a biblical principle where they allowed their land to rest for a whole year every seven years, and they reaped the most bountiful crops after that. I believe there is wisdom in letting the land recuperate. When planning your garden, keep these principles in mind.

Single-Bed Crop Rotation

Here's an example of what you might rotate in one garden bed and the sequence for planting. I also recommend learning which vegetables are related to one another—tomatoes, eggplant, and potatoes, for instance, are all in the nightshade family and are susceptible to some of the same pests and diseases. Avoid back-to-back planting of closely related crops in the same location.

- Year 1: Parsnips, beets, radishes, turnips, onions, garlic
- Year 2: Beans, peas, carrots, rosemary, sage, potatoes, corn
- Year 3: Brussels sprouts, lettuce, spinach, kale, cabbage, thyme, broccoli, cauliflower
- Year 4: Tomatoes, squash, cucumbers, peppers, celery, parsley, dill, basil

COMPANION PLANTING

One of my absolute favorite aspects of gardening is companion planting. It's amazing how plants can help each other. Just like finding the perfect friend, plants can impact each other's lives in a positive way. I've learned so much about relationships and friendships just by living in the country and being around animals and plants. When planting crops together, you can improve the soil, keep pests away, and create a beautiful garden. Companion planting is especially useful if you're growing in small spaces. You can interplant many different plants in a small area, and they will work together to keep each other healthy and thriving. It's like finding the perfect soil mate! By doing this, you won't have to worry as much about bugs taking over your garden, and your plants will thrive.

Tomatoes and basil make the perfect pair. Basil helps keep away flies and other pests, and both require similar amounts of sun and water. I like to plant my basil at the end of tomato rows or around my tomato cages or stakes. Another fun plant to add to this mix is marigolds. This is my absolute favorite combination and one I use all the time when planting my summer garden. Rosemary is known to repel cabbage moths, which love broccoli and other members of the Brassica family. Plant it between or in the middle of a group of broccoli to keep pests away.

Garlic makes a great companion for most veggies. It, too, helps deter pests and doesn't take up too much space. I like to interplant it and put it on the ends of my beds. My plants are always happy with this addition. Just be sure to not plant them near legumes such as beans and peas. Garlic will stunt their growth.

Onions and carrots are a great combination. Carrots are known to be attacked by the aptly named carrot fly, but these insects avoid onions, so planting them nearby really helps keep the bugs at bay. Other veggies that can suffer from the carrot fly are beets, cabbage, lettuce, and parsnips, so I plant those near onions, as well.

Corn, beans, and squash, known in many Native American cultures as the Three Sisters, have been planted together for centuries. The corn grows tall and offers the necessary support for the beans to climb up. The large leaves of the squash provide protection for the soil and keep it cool and moist, preventing weeds. Together, these three plants provide a perfect combination in the garden.

Winning Companion Planting Combinations

TOMATOES | BASIL | MARIGOLDS

BROCCOLI | ROSEMARY

BEANS | POTATOES

PEPPERS | CHIVES | PETUNIAS | GARLIC

EGGPLANT | THYME | SPINACH

CARROTS | ONIONS | RADISHES | MARIGOLDS

CABBAGE | DILL

SQUASH | NASTURTIUMS | MARIGOLDS | CORN

GARDENING AS A FAMILY

———

In my opinion, a garden should be not only a place to grow food but also a space where my family can come together and grow closer as a unit. As I plan my garden layout and design, I think about how we can utilize the space as an extension of our home. For instance, we could add a table and have dinner in the garden. The garden is a place where we can just be together, breathe in the fresh air, and connect with one another. I often joke with my husband that we now have garden dates. We'll spend time pulling weeds together while having some of the best life conversations.

The little ones could also have their own designated garden box or space. Planting together as a family is a wonderful way to create memories that we'll cherish forever. When it's time to start the seeds, I allow each family member to pick which vegetable they want to grow and care for in the garden.

Our activities don't have to be limited to just being in the garden. We can incorporate the joy of the outdoors into many aspects of our daily lives. For example, we can cook garden-to-table meals and enjoy them outside picnic-style.

My goal is to instill curiosity and a love of nature in my family. In today's world, where screens are everywhere, and our attention is always hooked on them, I want to reverse the narrative and make the outdoors the thing we long to see.

Involving Little Ones

From their first months of life, a baby can be brought into the garden to experience nature. As the child grows, they can more actively engage in what happens in the garden from day to day. I love to include the five senses when we do anything outside. Look up at the clouds and talk about their shapes. Touch the leaves of plants that are growing. Smell the flowers or dirt. Do you hear sounds in the garden, maybe a bird or a squirrel? Taste a basil leaf and tomato. Is it sweet?

As a parent, it's fun for me to also play along and think about these things. Don't be rushed; savor the ability to see, feel, and taste these wonderful treasures the garden brings. Try to make gardening a part of your daily family routine. Take time to create together—try the garden markers project on page 94. Make garden art together, place it in your garden, paint decorative birdhouses, have a harvest party. There are endless ways to grow together in the garden. On the next page, I've outlined a few ways you can easily garden together at any age.

Under one year of age:

- Let them shake unopened seed packets and hear the sounds.
- Have them pull grass, touch wood chips, and feel dirt.
- Place them under a tree to watch the leaves move in the wind.

Toddler:

- Help mix the water and soil for seedlings. It's messy but so very fun.
- Let your child help spray seedlings as they begin to grow. Check every day or two with them and watch their wonder and amazement as the first seedlings start to pop free from the soil.
- Taste test herbs. Herbs are such a fun part of the garden when you have children. Not only can your child enjoy the smell and texture, but the taste as well. While they help you harvest herbs , talk about the different smells, show them how to rub leaves between their fingers to enhance the scent, and see which tastes they like the best. Harvest and preserve some of those herbs together (see pages 142 and 144).
- Cook together with what you harvest. They can learn math and fine motor skills by helping you make a strawberry tart or watermelon salad (see page 171).

Ages four and older:

- By this age, they can determine between a weed and an actual plant. Have them help with light weeding in the garden
- Let them do some watering. The hose might be heavy, but kids will love watering the plants. Be encouraging, and just make sure they don't drown your plants.
- Let them choose some of what you'll plant. They have enough motor skills now to help direct sow seeds. Try varieties of peas and corn, which are easy to handle.
- As they grow older, kids can do some of the harvesting and planting all by themselves. Have them keep a gardening log and update it as the season passes. They will learn what did and didn't work and they can apply those lessons the next gardening season.

Grown-ups:

- Take your favorite book outside and read it in the garden. The fresh air and greenery will make your reading experience even more enjoyable.
- Invite friends and family over for a garden party. Enjoy food, drinks, and good company while surrounded by the beauty of your garden. See page 24 for more ideas.
- Set up a bird feeder or bird bath in the garden and spend some time observing the animals that come to visit. You might even attract some new species to your garden!
- Consider picking up a relaxing hobby that can be done in the garden, like painting or drawing. Natural beauty can inspire creativity.

GARDEN MARKER FAMILY ACTIVITY

Here is an easy garden-inspired activity we do as a family and it's fun for the little ones, too! I always try to label what I plant so I don't forget once it's all growing together. These little terra-cotta pots can be painted to match the veggie you're growing, or you can simply decorate them and write the variety's name on the inside. Use a pot size appropriate for each plant. It's a great afternoon garden activity.

YOU WILL NEED

Terra-cotta pots of various sizes

Damp cloth

Newspaper or tarp

Paper towels or rags

Acrylic paints in various colors, labeled for outdoor use

Paintbrushes of various sizes

Waterproof markers or paint pens

Clear sealant

Wooden skewer, chopstick, or stick

Instructions

Wipe the pots with a damp cloth to remove dirt and debris. Allow them to dry—it shouldn't take long.

Spread newspaper or a tarp to protect your work surface. Have paper towels or a rag on hand to keep any mess in check.

Paint the pots however you'd like. Get the whole family involved! Painting the inside is fine but won't be visible. Painting the rim of the pot may make it stick to surfaces as it dries.

Set the pots on the newspaper or tarp to dry thoroughly. No one wants their masterpiece smudged!

Use waterproof markers or pens to write the plants' names on the insides of the dry pots, one name per pot. Be sure to seal the pots prior to using them to ensure the paint does not wash off.

Push a stick into the ground next to each plant or type of plant (you don't need to label each in a row or group of the same plant).

Slide each pot onto the stick of its corresponding plant.

Enjoy all the cute little pots as you walk around your garden!

NOTE: USE THOSE LITTLE POTS TO START SEEDS IN DURING THE OFFSEASON.

WHAT *to* PLANT *in* YOUR GARDEN

O nce I learned more about gardening and got my hands in the soil, it was time to plan our first "real" garden. I ordered way more seeds than we could ever plant, varieties you've never heard of, and at the end of the season, I realized I never used half of them and honestly didn't enjoy some of what I did grow.

As you decide what to plant, consider what you and your family love eating. For us, it's lots of tomatoes, peppers, onions, garlic, cabbage, broccoli, carrots, and cucumbers. I select foods that we can enjoy not only when picked but also preserved to eat later. Yes, I do sprinkle other veggies in the mix and sometimes get a few random seeds, but for the most part, I stick with what we want to eat. I recommend you do the same.

I think one of the biggest mistakes a gardener can make is trying to grow too much food at once. While hundreds of tomato plants sound like a good idea, let me guarantee you it is not unless you have a good plan for when all those tomatoes begin to ripen. It's easy to start many seeds, but remember those seeds will grow into plants. Consider all the effort, maintenance, and harvesting it will take. Not to mention the space required to grow all those little plants.

Also, always check that you can grow the foods you love in your hardiness zone. I might sound like a broken record, but I promise it makes a difference.

PLAN FOR YOUR FAMILY

———

A few points to consider before planting:

· **How much space do you have?** For a family of four, you need an average of 300 to 500 square feet (28 to 46 sq m) of garden to supply your family with food. Plants such as tomatoes, peppers, and cabbage need about 12 inches (30 cm) of space around them to grow adequately. Remember, you can always grow vertically to give extra space when needed. You can calculate your own family's needs using www.omnicalculator.com.

· **How will you use what you grow?** Decide whether your produce will mostly be eaten fresh during the summer and fall, or if you want to grow enough to preserve some for the winter too.

· **Who will eat the foods you plant?** Of the foods your family loves to eat, decide which family members will partake of that food. For example, consider the difference between a toddler eating potatoes and a teenage boy eating potatoes. You'll want to plant many more potatoes if you have a hungry teenager in the home. Likewise, if only one person will eat a particular vegetable, keep that in mind as you decide how many plants you want.

If you have no idea how much of a certain food your family eats, keep a notebook in your kitchen and make a hash mark every time you eat that item. For example, every time you cut an onion, mark it down. Assuming your list reflects your typical habits, at the end of a week or two, you'll have a pretty good idea, on average, of what your family eats. You can then calculate how much your family would eat each month and multiply that by twelve to get an average for the year.

One goal I had a few years back was to grow enough tomatoes to can pizza and pasta sauce for the year. To do that, I started twelve seedlings of one of my favorite Roma tomato varieties, Martino's Roma. From July through September, we harvested tomatoes from those plants. I canned about 35 pints (17 L) and could have canned more had I kept up with the volume of tomatoes. I use about three or four pints a week of sauce, for pasta, pizza, etc. Those twelve tomato plants gave me enough sauce for three months. Amazing, right? Based on that, I know I need about forty-eight plants to produce enough sauce for a year!

What to Plant Per Person

There is no magic number regarding how many plants your family needs to have enough food during a growing season. These are just suggestions—and I added amounts for the ones we tend to preserve the most. Keep in mind you will need to plant more if you plan on preserving as well.

Apples 1 tree

Asparagus 5–10 plants

Beets 15–30 plants

Blackberries 1–2 bushes

Blueberries 3 bushes

Broccoli 3 plants (15 if preserving)

Carrots 48 plants (200 if preserving)

Cauliflower 3 plants

Corn 10 plants (25 if preserving)

Cucumber 1–2 plants (4 if preserving)

Garlic 10 plants (25 if preserving)

Onion 12 bulbs (50 if preserving)

Peach 1 tree

Peas 15–20 plants

Peppers 3–4 plants (9 if preserving)

Spinach 30 plants (60 if preserving)

Squash 1–2 plants

Strawberries 12 plants (35 if preserving)

Tomatoes 2–4 plants (9 if preserving)

and increase water retention. Growing perennial crops means spending less time replanting and more time enjoying the harvest. Over time, as the plants grow and mature, you'll have a larger and more consistent harvest, enhancing food security for your home.

There are so many wonderful perennial crops to choose from. Some of my favorites are strawberries, blueberries, raspberries, and blackberries, which provide delicious fruits and add beauty to the garden with their colorful foliage and blooms. Additionally, you can plant artichokes, asparagus, 'Kosmic Kale', radicchio, and rhubarb, which are low maintenance and add variety to your harvest. Some herbs, such as mint, thyme, parsley, sage, and oregano, are also perennial in many zones, adding the opportunity for fresh culinary flavors without yearly planting. Finally, the addition of fruit trees to my farm has proven incredibly beneficial. We have apples, cherries, peaches, pears, plums, and figs! If only I could grow lemons, avocados, and mangos here! Depending on where you live, though, you might be able to. Once established, perennial crops provide bountiful harvests year after year, offering a sustainable source of fresh fruit.

As I plan my garden, I consider how perennials can benefit my space and home. They are a wise choice for saving time, effort, and money while promoting sustainable gardening practices with their deep roots and long-lasting nature. They are a gardening investment that keeps on giving, season after season.

The Benefit of Perennials

I've always believed in the saying, "Work smarter, not harder," and this rings especially true when it comes to gardening. Perennial crops save time, effort, and money, making them a smart choice for gardeners. Why bother planting something year after year if you can just plant it once?

Unlike annuals, perennials don't need to be replanted every year. They devote their energy to growing deep roots that help prevent soil erosion

GARDENING THROUGH
THE SEASONS

———

Why hibernate through the winter when you can add color and life to your garden by planting things that will tolerate the elements? Make it a habit to get your hands in the soil year-round. Plant tulip bulbs in the fall, grow an herb garden by your windowsill in winter, and harvest fresh greens from your patio containers in the spring. Gardening is not just for those summer tomatoes; there is so much each season has to offer.

It's surprising how many plants can survive the bitter cold and snow. I remember walking through my garden one spring and clearing weeds in preparation for planting. I came across carrot tops amid a pile of weeds and couldn't believe it. They were a vibrant green and full of life after a long winter of snow and freezing temperatures. I pulled them to reveal the most beautiful, perfect roots. Carrots get sweeter with time, and these were some of the best I ever grew. I didn't even know they were there. You can enjoy year-round gardening in a variety of ways.

Microgreens

One of my favorite ways to garden year-round is by growing microgreens. You can get fresh vitamins and minerals by growing these in your home, no garden space necessary. Microgreens are young, tender veggie plants harvested when they're around 2 inches (5 cm) tall. Of those commonly used—broccoli, arugula, sunflower, and pea—radish is one of the easiest. Simply fill a tray with soil and mist it with water until it's moist. Sprinkle your radish seeds as evenly as you can across the entire tray. You'll use a lot of seeds. Wet again and then cover it so they're in the dark for a few days. Once they sprout, place them by a window and keep the soil damp but not soggy. After seven days, they will be the right size to harvest; simply use clean scissors to cut them off at soil level. Toss them in salads and sandwiches, or munch on them right away. Easy and packed full of nutrients, microgreens are great no matter what time of year you grow them.

Extending the Growing Season

It can be very disheartening to walk out to the garden one morning and see your beautiful plants darkened and wilting from a sudden late-night frost, especially if the weather jumps back up and is sunny for weeks after. When you live in a zone with weather unpredictability, consider some of the following ways to help extend your growing season.

Greenhouse. For me, the greenhouse has been a true place of peace, warmth, and joy during winter. On the coldest days, it is warm inside and full of life. A greenhouse is a structure that allows a controlled environment to grow plants. They come in many different sizes; some are seasonal and some can be used all year. In a greenhouse, you can start plants earlier in the spring and grow them later into the fall, extending your growing season even during harsh weather. Greenhouse kits can be purchased but are sometimes costly; however, you can create your own greenhouse from repurposed windows and frames. I found all my greenhouse windows online for $250 and we framed around them. Get creative, and you can have your garden oasis year-round.

Row Cover. Row covers are lightweight blankets made of a fabric of plastic that can be placed over the garden beds to help protect plants from cold temperatures, wind, and even pests, such as those that attack Brassicas. They can extend the growing season by several weeks to even months and are one of the easiest and least expensive ways to protect your garden.

Cold Frame or Hoop House. These simple structures are also used to protect plants from cold temperatures and wind. Made with PVC pipes, metal (for hoop houses), or wood and covered in plastic, they are usually light enough that you can move them around easily. They create a dome-like structure over your garden bed or in-ground garden to keep it warm and protected.

Mulch. Mulch helps regulate soil temperature and retain moisture. This is especially helpful with raised beds. We use seedless straw (not hay!) and leaves as mulch for ours. I love to mulch my beds heavily in the late fall or early winter, once frost has come. It's amazing in spring to pull back the mulch and see the rich, dark soil it has been protecting for months.

Containers. Container gardening lets you bring pots inside when the weather gets too cold. Herbs, tomatoes, peppers, salad greens, carrots, radishes, and scallions can thrive indoors if you keep them watered and warm by a sunny window. Fresh herbs add wonderful flavor to meals, and having them year-round can be such a treat.

THE HOME ORCHARD
AND BERRY PATCH

———

I have an absolute love for juicy blueberries, freshly picked during summer. Their natural sweetness makes them the perfect snack to enjoy on a hot, humid day. Living in Georgia, I am fortunate to have peaches native to my region. One of my fondest summer memories is when my family gathered so many peaches that we had a fresh supply for months. As the seasons transition to fall, our fruit trees are adorned with red and green apples and tart pears, offering a bountiful harvest from our backyard.

Growing a home orchard and berry patch can offer numerous benefits to your home. My favorite is the nutritious and yummy produce they offer me year after year. The fruit I harvest from my yard is grown organically, and I know my family is getting the freshest, healthiest produce around—without the pesticides used in conventional farming techniques. But beyond that, fruit trees are low maintenance and improve soil health with their deep root systems, which break up the compact soil. Their leaves provide homes for pollinators and other beneficial insects and animals, and, once those leaves fall, I can use them as mulch. You don't need hundreds of trees and acres of land to reap the benefits of an orchard. When I was growing up, my dad only had three trees in our backyard, yet we had bushels of pears each year. If you have limited space, investigate dwarf fruit tree varieties and berry varieties that do well in containers.

Apply the following principles when caring for your trees and bushes; you will see the benefits they bring you.

The Organic Orchard

Before chickens and gardens were on my mind, fruit trees were the first thing I focused on when moving to the country. Since they took years to truly establish, they were a priority.

An organic orchard can be tricky because pests and diseases tend to creep in and you want to avoid fixing the problem with synthetic products. Here are a few things that have helped keep my trees healthy and disease free.

Siting the trees in an area with good drainage sets them up for success and feeding them once a season with an organic fertilizer boosts the nutrients in their soil. Yearly pruning strengthens the plant, increases airflow among the branches, and allows sunlight to reach the interior of the tree's canopy. Perhaps what has helped most, though, is planting our trees around our vegetable garden. The garden is filled with plants like chives, mint, garlic, marigolds, and others that help repel pests. If you plant a solitary tree, consider adding herbs and other beneficial plants nearby.

Before you buy fruit trees, make sure they're appropriate for your zone, then research their pollination requirements. You'll need to know if they are self-fertile (the pollen they produce works on their own flowers) or if they need cross-pollination, which means they can only set fruit with pollen from a compatible variety. When I ordered our fruit trees, the company was very kind to explain which varieties would be best. Some of the apple varieties I wanted would not have pollinated correctly, and I would have never gotten fruit. Ask questions and ensure you know what to get before buying random fruit trees at the store. When planting our fruit trees, my husband followed a unique method he had heard of years before. The trees we planted this way have grown twice as big and fast as other trees we planted not using this method.

Planting a Fruit Tree

- Dig a larger hole than you think you'll need. For most of our trees, we made a hole that was 3 × 3 feet (1 × 1 m). This loosens all the soil so that the roots can easily inch their way left and right and down to find more nutrients to keep growing.

- Put a mix of very rich compost and topsoil into the bottom of your hole. You want the roots to reach down and find all the good stuff deep in this hole.

- Put a thin layer of gravel on top of this mixture—any type of rock will do; I'm told this does something to the electrical current in the ground and channels it into the tree.

- Fill just the ends of a 12-inch (30 cm) long piece of 4-inch (10 cm) PVC pipe with large rocks. The idea is to keep dirt from getting inside the middle of the pipe. The oxygen trapped inside it feeds microorganisms in the hole and, as they flourish, they boost the tree's growth. This sounds crazy, but I promise your trees will grow so much faster because of it.

- Place the pipe horizontally in the hole and gently add more of your mixture of soil and amendments until the hole is two-thirds full.

- Put a big rock (bigger than 4 inches [10 cm] across) on top of your mixture, add another little layer of your soil mixture on top of that rock, and then set your tree on top.

- Fill the rest of the hole around your tree with your soil mixture.

- Cover the soil with mulch, such as hay or straw.

- Water that tree for 10 to 15 minutes each day for the first two weeks.

- Watch your tree grow!

Tips for Trimming Fruit Trees

I was so excited to see blooms the first year we had our fruit trees and bushes, but out of nowhere my husband crashed my party by insisting we remove the blooms. This, of course, seemed counterintuitive. After all, flowers are the precursor to fruit, right? However, his reasoning was sound: He was following a biblical principle found in Leviticus. By plucking off the fruit buds each spring for the first three years, we allowed the tree to channel all its energy into developing deep, sturdy roots. This investment in early root growth paid off in the long run, as our trees and bushes flourished with abundant fruit and good health. They became more resilient to drought and disease as well. So, if you're planting trees or berries and have the patience for it, consider following this approach for optimal health and vitality. Here are some other tips for pruning your fruit-bearing plants:

- Trim off the smaller branches (side shoots) so you have branches that can hold the weight of the ripe fruit. It looks nice to have lots of fruit, but weak branches can break.
- Trim trees in the shape of an upside-down open umbrella—with the widest part being at the top. Trim out the middle, which helps the tree get lots of sunlight, helping to prevent disease.
- Remove any branches below about 3 feet (1 m) off the ground. This will make it easier to walk and mow around and under the tree.
- Trim the tops so the trees do not get taller than about 7 feet (2 m). This will allow you to reach all the fruit without losing any.

Berry Patch

Having your berry patch at home can be quite a rewarding experience. Since they are perennials, you only need to plant them one time, and year after year you'll harvest sweet berries. Choose a sunny spot with well-draining, acidic soil for your patch and select berry varieties that grow well in your region. Plant in the spring or fall, spacing them with plenty of room for airflow. Ensure they are watered properly, especially when first planted and during low rain seasons. Mulch around the plants with pine straw (fallen pine needles), which is naturally acidic and will help improve the soil. Berries like raspberries and blackberries tend to grow tall and wild, so consider using a trellis or some sort of support when planting. You can also plant them next to an evergreen or hydrangea, as they both benefit from acidic soil.

When it comes to blueberries, lowbush varieties produce small, sweet fruits ideal for making jams, jellies, cobblers, and more, while highbush varieties, such as Nelson or Jersey, tend to thrive in colder climates. In contrast, rabbiteye varieties, which turn pink before they ripen to blue, are vulnerable to cooler temperatures and frost. They are more popular in southern regions.

If you have limited growing space, strawberries are a wonderful option. Apart from growing them in a garden bed, you can plant them in hanging baskets or patio containers. If planting in a bed, be sure to space them about 18 inches (46 cm) apart so they have room to spread. June-, or summer-bearing, strawberries produce fruit over a specific time. Those that produce throughout the warmer months are known as everbearing.

When harvesting any berries, do so in the morning when the weather is cool and the plants are well hydrated from their overnight rest. This is typically when the sugar content in the berries is at its highest, resulting in the sweetest flavor!

FLOWERS IN THE GARDEN

———

Lady Bird Johnson once said, "Where flowers bloom, so does hope." A flower can grow and bloom through the thickest weeds; some need only be thrown onto dirt to sprout and grow. Flowers bring that extra oomph to a garden space and a smile to my face on the cloudiest day. Their aesthetically pleasing bright colors and shapes dance in the wind as I gather my harvests. They almost nod in approval of what I'm doing. I always knew I wanted to grow flowers, but I never truly understood the connection between them and the earth until I witnessed some of the ways flowering plants help my garden.

Benefits of Flowers

Pollination. If you want a successful garden, plant flowers. They are a crucial part of aiding pollination. Bees, butterflies, and other pollinators are attracted to flowers' bright colors and fragrances. They then transfer pollen from one flower to another—including your food crops—as they collect nectar.

Habitat. Flowers provide a home and habitat for beneficial insects and animals such as bees, butterflies, and hummingbirds.

Bee balm, coneflowers, black-eyed Susans, milkweed, sunflowers, and lavender are some of my favorite flowering plants that aid pollination and create habitat. If certain flower varieties are local to your area (often referred to as native plants), choose them, and they will help attract your local pollinators and insects. Choosing flowers that can bloom at different times throughout the growing season is important. This will ensure there is a consistent food source available.

Soil health. Flowers with particularly deep root systems, such as sunflowers, purple coneflowers, yarrow, milkweed, and black-eyed Susans, can help improve soil health by loosening compacted soil and increasing soil organic matter.

Medicinal benefits. Flowers have long been admired for their beauty and fragrance, but did you know many also have incredible medicinal properties? Chamomile, for example, is known for its soothing effects. I have used it to treat a stomachache and as a relaxing tea before bedtime to help me sleep. I've also used marigolds in creams and salves to treat minor skin rashes and irritations. If you're interested in flowers for their medicinal benefits, do a little research before starting your garden and see where you can incorporate these incredible blooms.

Education. I try to teach my daughter about things in nature and make them a topic of conversation every time we walk outdoors. Not only are flowers beautiful and fascinating, but they also offer important lessons and insights about various aspects of life, ones I didn't even realize or think about until I started growing them— protection, reproduction, connection, nurturing, growth, and renewal, to name a few. Flowers serve as a reminder of the wonders and intricacies of nature and can inspire us to appreciate and learn from the world around us.

Stress reduction. A study conducted at Rutgers University found that the presence of flowers led to happiness and feelings of satisfaction among study participants. I know they bring me stress reduction and joy whenever I go to the garden, and that alone is reason enough for me to plant them. I also believe in passing on to others the joy I have found in flowers and like to give them away to family and friends. You can also do this by sharing seeds you've saved from the flowers you grow. Living simply is about appreciating the little things; flowers are perfect for that.

Edible flowers. One of my favorite ways to add color and beauty to fresh garden dishes is by incorporating edible flowers. It's a great way to bring nature in and add a wow factor to your food. Toss nasturtium blooms into a salad for a peppery kick or dandelions for a bit of tang. Make chive blossom vinegar for your salad dressing (see page 31). Lavender blooms add a delicious flavor to baked goods, and pansy and rose make the tastiest popsicles. Wrap up your day with a soothing cup of chamomile tea. The possibilities are endless, and including flowers in your food gives you a few extra nutrients in your meals, too.

the scorching sun. Sunflowers can come to the rescue by providing much-needed shade when planted on the south or west side of your garden. Additionally, their seeds are a delicious treat when roasted or added to baked goods and granola. And have you tried sunflower seed butter? It's a delectable substitute for peanut butter. If you're interested in saving seeds for the next season, I recommend mammoth varieties of sunflowers. And don't forget: You can repurpose the stalks as garden trellises or support structures.

Cosmos. Cosmos are one of the best flowers to plant for several reasons. First and foremost, they are incredibly easy to grow and maintain, making them an ideal choice for novice gardeners. I have thrown flowers into the soil, and they've thrived without any added effort on my part. They are also prolific bloomers, producing large quantities of flowers throughout the growing season, with a wide range of colors, including pink, purple, red, and white. Their delicate petals and fern-like foliage add a graceful appearance to any garden. And they are a favorite for pollinators as well. They are the perfect cut flower and are beautiful when pressed to use for crafts or gifts.

Dahlias. I was instantly hooked the first time I saw a dahlia. Available in myriad shapes, colors, and sizes, they bloom from midsummer through your first frost, giving you a long season of gorgeous blooms. Mine welcome me into the garden with their bright colors and unique details. I guarantee they will provide you with instant happiness, in addition to plenty of bees, hummingbirds, and other pollinators. I love that they also have medicinal benefits. Use the petals in a soak for tired feet or apply crushed petals on insect bites or stings to get relief.

My Favorite Flowers to Grow

I am not going to lie; I am obsessed with flowers. There is something truly magical and soothing about seeing them sway in the breeze. Through the years, I have grown my share of flowers, and these are a few that stand out.

Sunflowers. Sunflowers are my top choice for an annual flower due to their versatility in the garden. Not only are they visually stunning, but they can also serve a practical purpose. For example, during the hot summer months, peas and beans may require some relief from

Full sun and well-draining soil are best for dahlias, but too much sun will cause them to suffer a bit, like during our hot Georgia summers. In warmer climates, they can be kept in the ground and grow back as perennials, but cooler climates will require you to dig up the tubers (the plant's root) and store them until the next season. Dahlias can be expensive, but if you take care of them, you won't have to buy new ones every year.

Many varieties grow quite large—they range in height from 15 inches to 6 feet (38 cm to 2 m) with flower diameters from under 2 inches to more than 10 inches (5 cm to 25 cm)—and have multiple stems that can become overcrowded, causing the flowers to fall. Tie them to stakes to help prevent them from growing wild and also give them a good trim before they bud flowers. This may seem like you're killing the plant, but pruning them back before they blossom will provide you with even more stunning blooms. Some of my favorite varieties are 'Café au Lait Royale', 'Café au Lait', 'Powder Puff Polka', 'Duet', 'Sylvia', and 'Fleurel'.

Zinnias. My absolute favorite cut flower, zinnias come in an array of colors and last over a week in a vase. If you are new to gardening, this is the flower for you! They are easy to grow, heat tolerant, low maintenance, and relatively pest resistant; best of all, butterflies and bees come in droves to feed on these beautiful flowers. How fun is it that I get to provide a little ecosystem for our pollinators amid the zinnias? I specifically love this flower because it's very easy to save the seeds and replant them again next year. Trust me, you'll have seeds to share with family and friends, and who doesn't want to grow beautiful flowers?

Only save seeds from open-pollinated zinnia varieties, which guarantees the blooms from those seeds will look the same as the parent plant, and only save from healthy blooms. To collect the seeds, simply let some of the flowerheads dry completely on the stem. Once they turn dark and withered, gently tap the head to remove the petals, and the seeds will be attached to the ends. They will look like little arrows. Store them in a cool, dry place. Saving just a few flower heads will give you enough seeds to plant a full garden the next year. My favorite varieties include 'Oklahoma Salmon', 'Lilliput Gem White', 'Peppermint Stick Mixed', 'Lilliput Salmon', and 'Bright Jewel Mix'.

Tips for Beautiful Blooms

Light. Most flowering plants require 6 hours of sunlight daily for healthy blooms, so site your gardens properly.

Water. Keep the soil moist but not waterlogged.

Deadhead. Regularly remove spent blooms to encourage new growth.

Prune. For roses and other perennial flowers, prune as needed to maintain shape and remove dead or damaged branches.

Support. Flowers with tall stems, like dahlias or sunflowers, might need the support of a stake or trellis to help them stand tall.

Feed. Use general organic fertilizer formulated for flowers to help add nutrition during the growing season. Some flowering plants, such as roses or hydrangeas, have more particular needs and there are fertilizers specifically designed for them.

POLLINATORS IN THE GARDEN

Pollination is crucial to producing fruits and vegetables. Without it, plants will not generate seeds or fruit, and the cycle of plant life will be unable to continue. Planting beautiful flowers and native plants will entice pollinators to come to you. Once they arrive, you can do a few things to encourage them to stay.

- **Provide water.** Pollinators need water for drinking and temperature regulation. You can add some rocks to a plant saucer and fill it with just enough water to cover the rocks to create a water station for your pollinators. Place it somewhere visible in your garden and watch them come take a drink.

- **Create habitat.** Help your pollinators by placing logs, branches, or hollow stems around your garden for them to use as a nesting site.

- **Avoid pesticides.** In our home and garden, we use only natural pesticides. Avoid harsh chemicals or products that disturb your garden's ecosystem and drive away beneficial creatures that could help you keep pests under control.

- **Provide shelter.** Planting shrubs and trees around your garden gives your pollinators a place to hide and shelter in extreme temperatures. You even can provide nesting boxes for bees.

In addition to the normal bumblebees and butterflies that pollinate the garden, I have added honeybees to our farm. They offer a better chance of adequate pollination, in addition to the delicious bonus of fresh honey. Although honey is the icing on the cake, for me, it's not about that. In keeping honeybees, I hope to offer an endangered species a safe and healthy environment to thrive while also increasing my garden's yield.

HERBS IN
THE GARDEN

———

I believe herbs are the "secret sauce" of a garden. They can help with pest control, offer medicinal properties, and make your food taste fresh and full of life. These aromatic herbs are easy to grow. Plant them in pots outside your kitchen for easy access or preserve them (see page 143) to extend their use past the growing season.

A Few Favorite Herbs
to Grow

- **Basil.** Have you ever had fresh pesto made with sweet basil that you picked minutes before? So much flavor and color! Basil is easy to grow, versatile in the kitchen, and attracts pollinators, making it a rewarding addition to any garden. Plant basil in well-drained soil, provide ample sunlight, water regularly, and pinch off flower buds to promote bushier growth and keep the basil from going to seed. I promise pinching the plant will cause it to grow quickly, and you'll have a never-ending supply of this amazing herb. My favorite varieties are Genovese (the classic basil used for pesto and recipes), Thai sweet, and lemon basil.

- **Rosemary.** Rosemary is a woody perennial herb known for its evergreen foliage. It can be grown as a shrub or a small tree, depending on the variety and growing conditions. While you can plant it in a pot or the garden, I realized you also could grow it as a shrub in certain zones when I noticed it in the landscaping at our church. Every spring, it has tiny purple and blue blooms that look stunning against the bright green foliage. With proper care, rosemary can thrive for many years, providing a consistent supply of fragrant leaves for culinary, aromatic, and other uses. The variety 'Spice Island' grows 3 to 4 feet (0.9 to 1.2 m) tall and is found at most local nurseries. It's very aromatic and perfect for cooking.

- **Lavender.** Lavender, in my opinion, is one of the most versatile herbs. Its visual appeal makes it a favorite to plant in my garden, but what I love most is that it is used in a wide range of applications. From culinary recipes and skin care to pest control, insect repellent, and cleaning products, the possibilities with lavender are truly endless. It's also excellent when dried for home décor products and DIY gifts. Even my chickens like it! I plant a mixture of English and Spanish lavender varieties at the ends of my garden beds, where the blooms add color and attract pollinators and the scent helps keep mosquitos, aphids, and rats away.

Tips for Trimming Herbs

- Begin to trim the herb as soon as the plant is strong and growing.
- Use clean, sharp snips to easily cut herbs and not damage the plant.
- Prune new growth about every week during the summer.
- Remove all the flower buds so the herbs last longer. Cilantro is an exception to this, as the seeds have culinary uses, too. (For the longest time, I had no idea that the spice coriander is cilantro seed!)

NATURAL PEST CONTROL

———

A healthy garden starts with healthy soil, but despite my best efforts, a pest or two always shows up. Here are some ways we control pests naturally in our gardens and orchard. I hope it helps you, too.

Companion planting. Certain plants, flowers, and herbs planted together can work at keeping disease away. Use this to your advantage and learn more on page 89.

Trap crops. A trap crop, also known as a decoy crop, helps lure in pests to keep them away from the main crop you want to protect. The pests will eat your trap crop and reduce the damage caused to the main one. Plant your trap crop near your main ones but not directly beside them. For example, nasturtium can lure aphids away from tomatoes and peppers. Japanese beetles love raspberries, so plant some a bit away from your garden. Yes, you'll sacrifice a few raspberries, but your garden will have fewer pests to control.

Pantry products. Consider using items from your kitchen pantry for natural pest control in your garden. A sprinkle of ground cloves in a planting hole can help deter mice, voles, and other rodents, while turmeric can be sprinkled in the planting hole to deter ants, slugs, and pill bugs. Add some cinnamon in your garden soil to deter rabbits, squirrels, and ants while also preventing fungus in seedling soil.

Best Plants for Pest Control

Flowers
Alliums
Chrysanthemums
Cosmos
Dahlias
Marigolds (French and Mexican)
Nasturtiums
Petunias
Sunflowers

Herbs
Basil
Borage
Catnip
Chives
Cilantro
Citronella
Dill
Eucalyptus
Garlic
Lavender
Lemongrass
Mint
Rosemary
Thyme

Animals in the Garden

People frequently ask me, "How do you prevent rats, mice, and other vermin from attacking your garden?" I have one simple answer: barn cats. That's right. My approach to managing my garden and farm is to bring in animals that can play a helpful role and reduce my workload. Our outdoor barn cats (currently five) are essential to our pest management plan. As a bonus, their quirky personalities provide some entertainment when we're out in the garden. Yes, at times, the cats might consider those lovely beds to be a litter box, but a few things can help prevent that:

- Don't leave garden boxes open with just dirt. Cats will most definitely use them as a litter box. Lay mulch, like straw or leaves, around your plants, which cats will be less likely to scratch and move around.

- Protect seeds and seedlings with chicken wire or a cloche. Once there's an established plant and mulch, cats leave the beds alone.

- Plant lavender to distract your cats. They don't like the smell. I planted lavender around most of my beds.

Ducks are excellent at foraging for pests and slugs, and their webbed feet prevent them from tearing up your garden. Unlike chickens, they just grab what they need without disturbing your space. They also can help with weed control by grazing on vegetation around your garden, leaving fertilizer wherever they go. For that and many other reasons, we introduced ducks to Azure Farm, and they have been such a wonderful addition.

I am also the proud caretaker of seven guinea fowl. Despite their occasional loudness, they have proven to be excellent insect controllers. They have a unique affinity for targeting pests, such as ticks, as well as the beetles and grasshoppers that can cause damage to crops and plants.

All in all, our cats, ducks, and guinea fowl, coupled with our gardening practices, have eliminated our need for pesticides.

HOMEMADE GARDEN PEST REPELLENT

Just because something says it's natural does not mean it's safe for your whole garden. Some store-bought natural sprays contain ingredients that can affect your pollinators and your garden's ecosystem. Here's an easy recipe for a garden spray that's harmless (unless you get it in your eyes) but gets the job done.

YOU WILL NEED

3 or 4 cloves garlic, finely chopped

1 tablespoon (6 g) cayenne powder

1 teaspoon neem oil, optional

2 cups (472 ml) water

Fine-mesh strainer

Cheesecloth or paper towel

16-ounce (472 ml) spray bottle

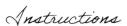

Instructions

Blend the garlic, cayenne, neem oil (if using), and water in a high-powered blender.

Refrigerate overnight.

Strain through a fine-mesh strainer lined with cheesecloth or a piece of paper towel. Do not omit this step. Any tiny particles will clog the spray nozzle.

Pour the seasoned water into a 16-ounce (472 ml) spray bottle.

Spray plants in the morning and evening, when pollinators are usually absent; reapply after rain. Be persistent, and over time, it will help. While the neem oil is optional, it has long been used safely for natural pest control. Just remember to use the amount directed; too much may harm your pollinators or cause other issues. Never spray flowers or any host plant of a pollinator and avoid spraying when pollinators are present.

GARDEN FAMILY ACTIVITIES

———

The garden offers countless opportunities for meaningful shared activities as a family. For instance, you could plant a tree or a berry bush every year and nurture it together while witnessing its growth. Work together to create a water station for pollinators and sow wildflower seeds, as they contribute to the flourishing of colorful blooms that attract and support these vital creatures. Imagine the satisfaction of gathering fresh basil from the garden and using it to make homemade pesto or adding a dash of lavender simple syrup (see page 126) to freshly squeezed lemonade. The possibilities are endless, and the garden becomes a hub of creativity, connection, and natural abundance for the family who gardens together. One of my favorite activities to do with my family is drying flowers from the garden and making pressed flower art to give as gifts.

PRESSED FLOWER ACTIVITY

Dried flower art is a great way to preserve summer flowers and enjoy them through the winter months. It also makes an extraordinary, beautiful gift. Low-moisture, freshly bloomed flowers work best, as they are less likely to discolor or mold. Drying them as soon after cutting as possible helps prevent browning. I like to use cosmos, lavender, daisies, poppies, zinnias, and herbs.

YOU WILL NEED

Fresh-cut flowers

Moisture-absorbing paper (printer paper, unwaxed cardboard, facial tissues; see Note, page 124)

1 or more books large enough to fit the flowers inside

Books or other heavy weight

Tweezers

Instructions

Remove any debris from the flowers with a good shake.

Place each flower between two sheets of absorbent paper. You can use the same sheets for multiple flowers, but the flowers should not be touching each other, as this can transfer moisture.

Put the paper-enveloped flowers between the pages of a book. Do not stack the sheets between the same pages.

Set the book in a place where it won't be disturbed, then put lots of weight on top of it.

Allow 2 to 3 weeks for the flowers to dry.

Gently separate the sheets of paper and remove the dried flowers with tweezers.

NOTE: AVOID USING PAPER TOWELS OR PARCHMENT PAPER.

Frame your dried flowers or use them for bookmarks, coasters, and cards—anything you can dream up! The possibilities are endless, and they make for a very thoughtful gift.

LAVENDER SIMPLE SYRUP

Lavender syrup is like a bottle of garden essence, with sweet floral notes that can freshen teas and lemonades. But it's not just for drinks; pour it over pancakes and waffles for a delightful alternative to maple syrup. You can even add it to a cake glaze or some whipped cream for a light and fresh dessert topping. Plus, making lavender syrup is incredibly easy and it makes a thoughtful gift.

YOU WILL NEED

1 cup (200 g) granulated sugar or coconut sugar (see Note)

1 cup (236 ml) water

1 tablespoon (3 g) fresh lavender buds or 1 teaspoon (5 g) dried culinary lavender buds

Instructions

Combine the sugar, water, and lavender buds in a small saucepan over medium-high heat. Bring it to a boil, stirring until the sugar dissolves.

Reduce the heat and simmer for 1 minute.

Remove from the heat and let the syrup steep for about 30 minutes.

Pour the syrup through a mesh strainer into a glass mason jar. Discard the solids.

Let the syrup cool before placing a lid on the jar.

Store in the refrigerator and use within 4 weeks.

NOTE: YOU CAN DOUBLE OR TRIPLE THIS RECIPE. ALWAYS USE A 1:1 RATIO OF SUGAR TO WATER. COCONUT SUGAR WILL DARKEN THE SYRUP AND MAKE IT A BIT CLOUDIER, BUT IT WILL NOT IMPACT THE TASTE.

PRESERVING
the HARVEST

There's nothing quite like picking fresh produce and eating it straight from the garden. Those vibrant cherry tomatoes, juicy and sweet, are pure heaven to snack on when it's hot outside. There is, however, something possibly even more exciting: enjoying their flavor in the dead of winter when there's frost on the ground and not a live veggie plant in sight.

That is one of many reasons why I love preserving food, but I think the main one is that I want my family to enjoy delicious, healthy food that's never been touched by dyes or preservatives. Knowing exactly where our food comes from and what's in it is something we should keep at the forefront of our minds. Enjoying homemade salsa, making delicious blueberry sauce, and seasoning your guacamole with homemade garlic powder is empowering and fun. You will realize you're making fewer trips to the grocery store because you're learning to be more self-sufficient.

I wish someone had told me years ago that I didn't need to live in the country or even have a garden to learn about food preservation. A garden helps, but you can source food from a farmers' market or local farm. All you need is the desire to do it and the bravery to take that first step.

My favorite ways to preserve food are canning, freezing, and dehydrating. The joy I find in preserving the foods I grow is only surpassed by the satisfaction of sharing that healthy, homemade food with others. It means so much to them, too, and spreads the ethic of simple living.

In this chapter, we'll take a tour through the unique methods of preserving and you'll also find a selection of my favorite recipes starting on page 154.

CANNING

If you didn't grow up with someone in the family who canned, you might think canning is reserved only for the home cook with years of experience. Or you may feel only someone with acres of land and gardens can enjoy it. I assure you this is not the case.

Canning is simply a method of preserving food by placing it in a sealed container (usually a glass jar) and heating it to a temperature high enough to kill any bacteria or other microorganisms that may be present. This process creates a vacuum seal, which prevents air and bacteria from entering the jar and spoiling the food. It is an effective way to preserve various foods, including fruits, vegetables, and even meats.

The two main methods of canning are water bath and pressure. Water-bath canning is used for high-acid foods such as fruits and pickles. The jars are filled with the food and then heated in a large pot of boiling water. The heat from the boiling water is high enough to kill bacteria and create a vacuum seal. Low-acid foods, such as vegetables and meats, require the higher temperatures a pressure canner produces to kill bacteria.

Low and High-Acid Foods

Low-Acid Foods

- Fish
- Meat
- Mushrooms
- Poultry
- Seafood
- Soups
- Vegetables (such as beans, corn, potatoes)

High-Acid Foods

- All fruits except bananas, melon, papaya, and watermelon
- Jam
- Jelly
- Pickled condiments
- Pickled veggies
- Olives
- Salsa with additional acid
- Tomato sauce with additional acid
- Tomatoes with additional acid

Canning Fears Addressed

When you can for the first time it's okay to have some reservations and concerns. Will you get sick from eating the food? Will the jars break? Did you follow the steps correctly? Once you know how to can safely, your fears should dissipate.

One of the biggest concerns when canning is botulism. Botulism is an illness caused by a type of bacteria called *Clostridium botulinum*. The amount of acid in a recipe is a key factor in determining what method is appropriate for producing safe canned food. Water-bath canning reaches a temperature of 212°F (100°C), which is sufficient to kill the bacteria that causes botulism in high-acid foods, but low-acid foods require the 240°F (116°C) reached by a pressure canner. If you follow a tested recipe from a reputable source and use the correct canning method, botulism won't be an issue.

Breaking jars is something that worried me as I started canning, but it's easy to avoid by warming the jars before filling them. You never want to put hot contents into a cold jar. Likewise, ease the temperature transition on the other side of the process. When removing the jars after processing, always place them on a towel or wooden cutting board—and never on a cold surface. Follow these standards, and your risk of breaking jars will go way down!

NOTE: FOLLOW THE MANUFACTURER'S GUIDELINES IF YOU ARE CONCERNED ABOUT YOUR PRESSURE CANNER EXPLODING. MODERN MODELS TEND TO HAVE BUILT-IN SAFETY MEASURES TO PREVENT THIS. I SUGGEST STARTING WITH SIMPLE WATER-BATH CANNING RECIPES IF YOU ARE NERVOUS ABOUT PRESSURE CANNING.

When canning, always use tested, proven recipes and follow all the steps; many mistakes are made because a recipe is not followed precisely. Ball® home canning has been my go-to for tested recipes and information. As an ambassador for the brand, I have learned all the ins and outs of canning and have found their recipes to be the very best. Included in this book are recipes I have adapted from original Ball home canning recipes (see page 154).

Canning Isn't Scary

My love for preserving food started many years ago, long before I had a beautiful garden and bountiful harvests. I was six and in a small, rural West Virginia kitchen with my Aunt Marty. It was Thanksgiving, and she was making green bean casserole, cornbread, apple crisp, and her famous stuffing. All the produce came from her large garden nestled in the mountains. Growing and preserving food was part of her DNA.

She said to me, "Annette, run down to the basement and grab me a jar of green beans, please." The basement was just what you would expect: dark, damp, and filled with antiques and boxes. Her canning jar closet was way down in the back corner. There were rows and rows of jars filled to the brim with pickles, sauces, and jams that Aunt Marty grew, harvested, and canned. The

wooden shelves had flower-patterned liners and each section of jars was labeled in her beautiful cursive handwriting.

The first time Aunt Marty visited my country home, I proudly showed her my homegrown tomatoes. I had little experience gardening or canning, but the thought of having fresh pizza sauce in the middle of winter was quite motivating. When she talked about canning, the process did not seem scary or complicated. She walked me through the steps with such a graceful and effortless flow. At that moment, I began to understand the benefits of country living—she shined the light on my calling to this simpler life. Preserving my harvest is now something I love to do and I hope to instill that same love for it in you.

Essential Canning Supplies

To can successfully and make the process easier, be sure you have the correct supplies on hand before you start.

Jars. Your recipe will indicate the appropriate jar size. In general, jams, jellies, and preserves go in ½-pint jars (8 ounces [227 g]), while pint jars (16 ounces [454 g]) are ideal for salsas, sauces, relishes, and pie fillings. You'll most likely use quart jars (32 ounces [908 g]) for fruits and vegetables. Jars come in two different opening sizes, regular and wide-mouth.

Canners. If you are canning high-acid foods, you can use a water-bath canner. There are standard water bath canners available for purchase, or you can use a large kitchen pot. Just ensure your pot is deep enough to cover your jars by 2 inches (5 cm) without boiling over.

Pressure canners are more complicated but you must use one to safely can low-acid food. If you use a vintage pressure canner, make sure it's in good working order. Modern versions are safer and more reliable, ranging in price from about $50 to $500 or more. **Note:** Pressure *cookers* are not the same thing as pressure *canners*, although some are capable of both functions. Programmable pressure cookers and multicookers are *not* designed for canning and will not reach the necessary temperatures for food safety.

Additional supplies. You will also need:

- *Jar lifter.* This pair of specialized tongs securely grips the jars so you can safely move them in and out of the hot water.

- *Headspace/bubble-remover tool.* Safe canning practices require that you leave a bit of empty space at the top of each jar and that you remove any bubbles from inside. This tool helps you do both.

- *Funnel.* Canning is sometimes a messy process, but using a funnel can help you be a little neater when you're ladling food into hot jars.

- *Trivet.* Included with any water-bath or pressure canner kit, this device keeps your jars from touching the bottom of the pot, where the concentrated heat could shatter them. If you don't have one, they are inexpensive and necessary for safe canning.

Basic Canning Steps

Always follow the directions of your recipe. The steps here are to give you an idea of the general process.

1) Wash your jars, bands, and lids in hot, soapy water or run them through the dishwasher.

2) Fill your canner with water and place it over medium heat.

3) Place your jars in the canner over medium-high heat to warm. If a recipe requires a lot of prep time, you can wait and warm the jars once you are closer to actually using them.

3)

4) Dry your lids and bands with a clean cloth and set them aside.

5) Prepare your foods according to recipe directions.

6) Use the jar lifter to empty a jar (pour the water back into the canner) and remove one hot jar from the canner.

7) Transfer the hot food you prepared into the jar, using a funnel to minimize spills. Fill only one jar at a time.

7)

8) Leave the amount of headspace recommended by the recipe.

9) Release excess air by pressing the contents toward the center of the jar with a bubble-remover tool. This is especially important when using a pressure canner.

10) Wipe the rim of the jar with a clean, damp towel, especially when working with sticky foods, such as jams or jellies. The rim must be clean for the jar lid to seal properly.

Continued

8)

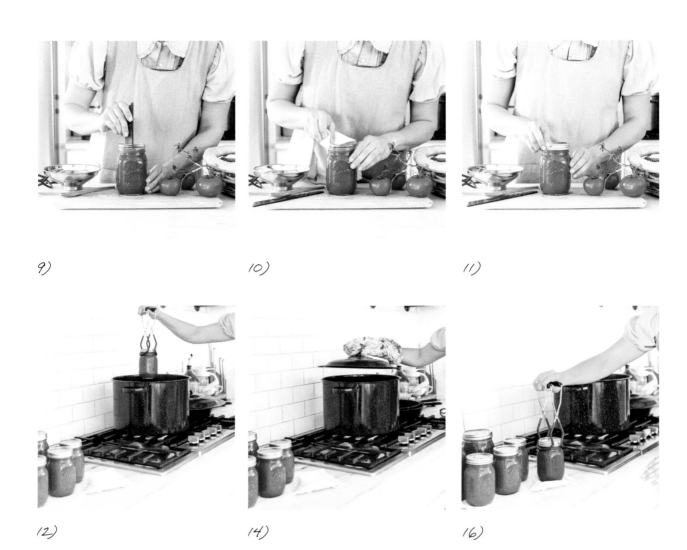

9)

10)

11)

12)

14)

16)

11) Center the lid on the jar, add a ring, and screw it on to just fingertip tight. **Do not over-tighten the lid.**

12) Carefully lower the jar into the water in the canner, using the jar lifter.

13) Repeat the steps until you've filled all the jars and placed them in the canner.

14) Place the lid on the canner and turn up the heat. Once the water begins to boil, set the timer as instructed in the recipe.

15) When the time ends, turn the heat off, remove the lid, and let it sit as instructed in the recipe, then remove the jars with the jar lifter.

16) Place the jars on a towel or a wood cutting board to cool, untouched, for 12 to 24 hours. If they sealed properly, the lids on the jars should not flex when pressed after that amount of time.

Canning Tips

- Always follow a recipe that comes from a reputable source.

- Have your food prepped and ready to go before you begin the canning process. This will save you a lot of time and stress and help prevent mistakes.

- To safely can, you need to have a specific amount of acid in a recipe. Do not alter the amount indicated by the recipe in any way.

- The acidity in fresh lemon juice may be inconsistent, so always use bottled lemon juice.

- Always warm the jars before filling them with anything hot.

- Leave processed jars undisturbed for 12 to 24 hours so they seal properly.

- For jams and jellies, know that you can safely reduce the amount of sugar in a recipe, but you may end up with a less desirable consistency.

- When canning salsa, you can swap out different types of peppers or onions without affecting the safety of the recipe.

- White vinegar can be safely swapped for apple cider vinegar as long as it has a 5 percent acidity.

- Canning can be pretty messy, so have lots of kitchen towels nearby.

- Marking each step as I go helps me keep track of where I am in a recipe without missing anything.

BLANCHING

Most vegetables need to be blanched before freezing, which helps slow down some of the enzyme breakdown in the food. My mother-in-law grows some of the most delicious corn in the summers and has a "put up your corn day." She blanches ears of corn, cuts the kernels off the cob, and then places them in bags to freeze. It's quite the process, but I have to tell you she has some of the most delicious, sweet corn because she blanched it. Depending on the vegetable, you'll steam blanch or use boiling water. After blanching, you may be directed to use an ice bath to help stop the cooking process. Getting everything trimmed and ready to go will make the process much smoother.

The best vegetables for steam blanching with an ice bath are asparagus, broccoli, cauliflower, corn, green beans, and okra. Cabbage and carrots do not require an ice bath. Peas do best with the boiling blanching method with an ice bath. For the most part, fruit is much easier and usually does not require special preparation.

Instructions

Bring a large pot of water to a boil.

Add a steamer insert, if you are using one.

Prepare an ice bath, if necessary. All you need is a large bowl filled with equal parts water and ice.

Chop the washed vegetables into pieces between ⅛ and ½ inch (3 mm and 1 cm) thick. Place them into the water and cover the pot. If you are using the steamer insert, cover the pot when it is full of steam.

Set your timer appropriately for what you're blanching.

When the timer rings, immediately drain the pot or remove the steamer insert and place the veggies in the ice bath, if you're using one.

Allow the vegetables to cool and dry before placing them into containers and freezing them.

FREEZING

When it comes to preserving food, freezing is one of the simplest methods. It requires no fancy steps or added ingredients. It gives you the freedom of long-term food storage while maintaining the quality and taste of many types of food. Freezing allows the flavor to get locked in and taste just as yummy months later when thawed while also maintaining nutritional benefits. Frozen food can keep for about six months to a year, which gives you enough time to eat it all before you freeze more.

Containers for Freezing

The best way to freeze large amounts of food is in freezer bags. You can lay them flat and label them properly, making your life a whole lot easier. I use them for all my larger and bulkier fruits and vegetables, but not for anything that is cooked or liquid. Always remove as much air as possible from the bag before freezing. Turn the bag on its side, flatten the produce as much as possible, and push the air out before quickly closing the seal. You can also suck the air out with a straw.

Some things, like soup and vegetable stock, I like to freeze in jars because it's easy and less messy than bags. However, not all jars are freezer safe. A good jar for freezing should have no shoulders, meaning the jar must go straight up and down with no change at the top. If there are shoulders, the jar is not freezer safe. Always leave plenty of headspace at the top of the jar and place it in the refrigerator to cool before placing it upright in the freezer until frozen solid.

Rigid plastic containers work for sauces, jams, and things of that nature. Use molds, such as ice cube trays or silicone molds, to freeze small amounts, then pop them out of the mold and into a freezer bag. Vacuum sealing is an option as well, but it can be expensive. You can achieve similar results without the fancy equipment.

Tips for Freezing a Few of My Favorites

Blueberries

Blueberries are an absolute favorite around here. They are the jewels of summer and the perfect snack on a hot day. Sadly, they're only in season for a few months. That's where freezing comes in handy. Blueberries are simple to freeze because they don't require any special preparation.

Don't wash them first. This might sound strange, but blueberries have a protective coating around them. If you wash them before freezing, they will not keep as well. (You can rinse them right before using them, instead.) Place them in a single layer on a cookie sheet and freeze them for about 2 hours. Transfer them to an airtight bag, label them, and place them back in the freezer until ready for use.

Other produce you can freeze this way are berries, cherry tomatoes, and peaches. I have a delicious and easy-to-make blueberry recipe sauce on page 160. It's perfect for a family brunch.

Peppers (Onions and Garlic, Too!)

Peppers, onions, and garlic are some of the easiest kinds of produce to freeze and are an excellent way to add flavor to recipes.

Wash the peppers first, then cut away the flesh from the stem and the seeds. Dice, thinly slice, or halve them—however you prefer them cut for using later. Pat them dry with a paper towel and transfer them to a baking sheet, spreading the pieces apart so they touch as little as possible. Place them in the freezer for 1 hour, then transfer them to a labeled, airtight bag or container. Remove as much air as possible before sealing and putting it back in the freezer.

This same process also applies to onions and garlic. Simply peel them first, then follow the above steps to freeze them.

Tomatoes

The freezer is a much-overlooked tool for preserving tomatoes. If you plan to use them in the depths of winter for sauces and stews, then freezing is a wonderful option. You can skip the puréeing and canning and just place them straight into freezer bags. Their delicious bright flavor will still shine through when you cook them months later, and you'll think you've gone back to July. You also have the added benefit of having the peels come right off when you thaw them, which is extra handy if you plan to can them later.

Rinse the tomatoes and pat them dry. Remove any green stems and use a paring knife to remove the woody core from the top. Place the tomatoes in a labeled, gallon-size (128 ounces [3.7 kg]) freezer bag and remove as much air as possible from the top before tightly sealing the bag. Lay the bag flat to freeze, then thaw as needed for a recipe or canning.

Herbs

Herbs are something you can grow in abundance even if you only have a small space. When you have a surplus, freezing is a great way to have that fresh taste available year-round. Basil is synonymous with summer and high on my list of what to preserve, but it tends to burn in the freezer. Coating it with olive oil can help and also makes it easier to break off when needed. For every 2 cups (46 g) of packed fresh basil, add ½ to 1 tablespoon (7 to 15 ml) of extra virgin olive oil and gently toss until evenly coated. Pack the leaves into a quart-size (32 ounces [908 g]) freezer bag, remove as much air as possible, and freeze immediately. Just break off a piece and toss it into your favorite recipe when cooking.

Other herbs, such as chives, cilantro, dill, oregano, rosemary, and sage, don't need special preparation. Simply rinse, dry, and chop them before placing them in a labeled container for use as needed.

For a quick way to add flavor to sauces or vegetables, freeze herbs in cubes with olive oil. Chop up your herb of choice and add it to an ice cube tray. Top with extra virgin olive oil and freeze. Keep the cubes in a labeled freezer bag. This works well for minced garlic, too.

DEHYDRATING

———

As a child, I remember dehydrating figs with my dad. It was such fun to pick fresh figs and load them into the dehydrator. Figs are just one of many foods that will keep for about a year when dehydrated—and some can last even longer if done correctly. That's because the process of dehydrating removes the moisture and liquid from the food, which prevents bacteria from growing and spoiling it. There are four popular methods for drying food.

Air-drying. You'll need a well-ventilated indoor space to air dry herbs, flowers, and some peppers. I love tying bunches of lavender and rosemary to dry for later use. Air-dry flowers and herbs in the dark to help retain their color and flavor. Some peppers, such as cayenne, are possibly the easiest of all to preserve. Simply place them on a sunny windowsill. Once they get crispy from the sun, remove the tops and stems. Crush what's left and you have red pepper flakes.

In the oven. Your home oven can be used for dehydrating if it goes down as low as 150°F to 170°F (66°C to 77°C). Open the oven door a bit to provide ventilation, allowing for humidity to escape.

Sun drying. You can use the power of the sun to dehydrate some foods. I know quite a few friends who do this routinely for sun-dried tomatoes. Placing a tray inside your car in the summer heat can speed up the process. Personally, I don't find this to be reliable enough to use as a go-to method, but it can still be a fun project to try with the family on a hot day.

Dehydrator. My preferred method, a dehydrator allows you to dry things at a specific temperature for a set amount of time. You can dehydrate a lot at once, and the results are even and consistent.

Dehydrating Supplies

Once you determine your dehydration method, you will need additional kitchen essentials.

- Trays or sheets for the dehydrator or oven
- Food to be dehydrated
- Knife and cutting board for preparing the food
- Storage for the finished product

A vacuum sealer for storage is nice but optional. I like to use canning jars to package most of my dehydrated items. Just be sure to use something with an airtight lid.

Tips for Dehydrating

- Cut foods to a uniform size and shape so they dry evenly. Doing it correctly from the beginning will help you have successful results.

- Like freezing, many vegetables should be blanched or cooked before dehydrating to help retain flavor and color. Asparagus, broccoli, cabbage, carrots, cauliflower, corn, okra, peas, peppers, and potatoes benefit from blanching.

- When it comes to some fruits, pretreating them with an acidic solution helps keep their colors bright and soften tough skin. Lemon is my pretreat of choice. Mix equal parts lemon juice and cold water, then allow the fruit to soak for 10 minutes. Drain well and pat dry before dehydrating. This is especially helpful with apples, apricots, nectarines, peaches, and pears.

- Always place the food in a single layer on the tray and make sure nothing overlaps.

- When dehydrating fruit, spray the tray with nonstick cooking spray first.

- One way to ensure you have successfully dehydrated something is to take it out of the dehydrator while still warm, place it in a jar, and close it. If, after 30 minutes or so, any moisture is seen on the food or jar, it is not dry enough and needs to be dehydrated for longer.

- Condition your dehydrated food by placing it in an airtight container and shaking it around once a day for about a week. If this doesn't produce moisture, store the food. If you *do* see any moisture, dehydrate the food more and repeat the conditioning step.

Two to Try First: Garlic and Apples

Dehydrating garlic is a great way to preserve the flavor and nutrition of this amazing spice. Peel the cloves and slice them very thin or chop them well; do not use a food processor to do this, as it may make more of a garlic paste, which you do not want.

Spread the sliced or chopped garlic in a single layer on a dehydrator tray or oven sheet. In a dehydrator, it will take approximately 6 to 8 hours (be sure to follow the manufacturer's guidelines for the dehydrator you are using). If you are using your home oven, try drying it at about 140°F (60°C). Every 30 minutes or so, turn the garlic with a spatula and spread it into a thin layer once more. It takes about 3 hours and will be darker than if you use a dehydrator, but it will still be good.

Once dehydrated, you can make garlic powder by placing the dehydrated garlic pieces in a food processor or coffee grinder until it becomes a fine powder. Store it, or the larger pieces, in an airtight container and enjoy it in your soups, sauces, marinades, and more!

If you're in the mood to try something sweet rather than savory for your first dehydrating project, apples would be my pick. They are easy and make a yummy addition to so many recipes, as well as a granola topping (see page 186)—or eat them straight from the dehydrator as a snack!

Peel and core your apple and slice it into ⅛- to ¼-inch-thick (3 to 6 mm) rings. Use the lemon juice pretreat from Tips for Dehydrating (see page 145) to prevent the slices from browning. Place the slices on the dehydrator tray or oven sheet in a single layer. Run the dehydrator at 135°F (57°C) for about 12 hours or until fully dry. If you are using your home oven, set it to 140°F (60°C) or the lowest possible setting. Keep the door open a bit for ventilation so moisture can escape. Turn the apples every hour and watch them closely; it's easy to burn them. The process should take 2 to 4 hours. Condition your apples as described in Tips for Dehydrating (see page 145) to make sure they are completely dry. Try not to eat them all before storing them—they are just that good!

NOTE: FOLLOW THIS SAME PROCESS FOR ONIONS. SIMPLY CUT THEM INTO SMALL PIECES OR THIN RINGS, DEHYDRATE THEM, AND THEN PROCESS THEM INTO A FINE POWDER, IF DESIRED.

— SEED SAVING —

I would have never thought of saving seed as a way of preserving my harvest, but the first year we lived on the farm I planted some cantaloupe from seed that was gifted to me. It was the most delicious cantaloupe I've ever tasted: they were so sweet and they melted in my mouth. I knew I wanted to save those seeds so I could grow them again the following year.

Seed saving preserves the genetic diversity of plants and it's a cost-effective method to have more plants for future growing seasons. For thousands of years, farmers saved some of their seeds each year so that they could plant the following year. Saved seeds are an investment in your garden's future.

Years ago, I heard of a school out in the western United States that would give the students a cob of corn to go out and start a new life. They would take that cob and use all the kernels to plant corn the following season. Those 200 kernels turned into 200 plants, each with four or more corn cobs. That one cob had turned into 160,000 kernels of corn in just one year! Imagine the increase year after year by saving just a small portion of kernels for seed. How fun is that?

Before You Start Saving Seed

The type of seed does matter. I wish it were as easy as saving seeds from your favorite veggies, but there is a little more science to it. Only save seeds from plants, such as peas, beans, tomatoes, and peppers, that can self-pollinate, which means they have all the parts necessary in the flower itself to reproduce. These are the easiest to save because it is less likely they will have crossed with other varieties in the garden. The seeds of these plants will usually grow to resemble the original fruit the most and produce a reliable result.

Within the self-pollinating category, we categorize plants as hybrid and open-pollinated. Humans develop hybrid varieties for disease

resistance, high yield, and such; there's no guarantee the seeds you collect from hybrid plants will grow into a plant with similar characteristics. Seeds from open-pollinated, also known as heirloom, varieties, on the other hand, should produce plants with the same characteristics as the parent plant. I try to grow only heirloom varieties and I find it amazing to get the same result and taste every year because of it. See chapter 3 for more information.

Bottom line? Know the plant whose seeds you want to save—and bet on heirlooms!

Harvest from plants with "wet" seeds, such as tomato, eggplant, cucumber, and such, when the fruit is ripe, and process them to remove the pulp and gelatinous coating surrounding the seed. To do this, scoop out the seeds of fully ripe fruit and put them in a glass jar with a bit of water. Keep them in there, stirring a couple of times a day, for 3 to 4 days to allow the mixture to ferment. Viable seeds will sink to the bottom. Strain them out, rinse them, and set them on a paper towel to dry. Then, transfer them to something they won't stick to, such as a dinner plate. Place them in a warm, dark place for 2 to 3 weeks to dry out thoroughly.

If you are collecting seeds from a "dry" plant such as peas and beans, the seeds should be left inside their pods until they are brown and dry and the seeds are rattling. Remove the pods from the plants and spread them out indoors in a dry place out of sunlight. After a couple of weeks, shell the pods to remove the seeds.

The seed heads of many flowers and herbs must turn dry and brown before it's worth it to collect them. My favorites to save are zinnias. Leave them on the stem until they are fully dry and you'll have hundreds of seeds from just a few blooms.

Store your seeds in a cool, dry place in airtight containers. Paper envelopes or a glass jar with a tight-fitting lid are good options. I keep mine in large photo storage containers so I can view them easily. Organize them as you see fit— alphabetically or by plant date are only two possibilities. Every season, take inventory so there are no surprises when the next planting season arrives.

Tips for Seed Saving

Choose healthy plants and allow the seed heads or fruit to fully mature before harvesting them. The plants should be disease-free with good genetics to ensure that the seeds you save will be strong and produce healthy plants in the future.

Wait until the seeds are fully mature and ready to be harvested before collecting them. If you harvest too early, the seeds may not be fully developed and may not germinate. The key to successfully doing this is knowing which seed-saving method you will use.

WAYS TO INCLUDE THE FAMILY WHEN PRESERVING THE HARVEST

————

A few summers back, I harvested about forty tomatoes and decided to make barbecue sauce. It took me four hours from start to finish and yielded one jar. Just one! For a moment, it felt like a complete waste of my time. Then I realized something: I had spent those four hours with my three-year-old daughter by my side. She helped gather the tomatoes and watched as I carefully peeled and cooked them. It took longer because her tiny hands and feet needed my attention. I will never forget these sweet memories with her in the kitchen. Though one jar is not a lot, the lessons I learned from that jar will forever be a part of my story.

Preserving food might feel antiquated and irrelevant to some. We have so many modern-day conveniences that it might seem silly to put in so much effort when you can just buy that jar of sauce at a store. However, you will learn much about yourself and enjoy preserving some of your food. You will feel a sense of pride in what you do. The values you learn from food preservation will be tangible every time you open a jar. I hope you can experience the same joy I have. Start learning about food preservation now. Don't wait until the perfect scenario arrives. Take control of where your food comes from and reap all the benefits it will bring you and your family.

Memorable Moments

In your home garden, involve the family from the very beginning. Have the little ones help plant cucumber seeds. As they watch the seeds sprout and grow, tell them those little plants will soon become delicious crunchy pickles, and then involve them in making that happen (see page 156). When picking tomatoes, talk about turning them into delicious tomato sauce.

If you don't have a garden, no problem. Go to a local blueberry farm in the summer and fill your buckets with fruit. Bring the whole family—aunts, uncles, cousins, and grandparents—and make it an event. They can then all join in the process of preparing and packaging them for the freezer. If blueberries are classic to summer, apple picking must be the fall equivalent. Make applesauce and dehydrated apples together. Yes, it will take you longer when others get involved, but the values you'll teach and the memories you create will be worth it.

Preserving the Harvest with Little Ones

Kids can get involved in preserving as early as 18 months in some cases. No matter what type of preservation you're doing, they can watch, learn, and be included.

General

- Pick produce from the garden.
- Rinse the fruits and vegetables.
- Use a child-safe knife to cut soft fruits and veggies.
- Label the food you preserve.

Canning

- Fill the jars with measured-out ingredients.
- Stir ingredients.
- Help read the recipe.
- Learn the importance of food safety.
- Learn how to follow steps.
- Measure headspace.
- Make pickles together.

Freezing

- Help remove food from the ice bath and pat it dry.
- Lay out food on a tray to flash freeze before placing it in bags.
- Package the food in freezer-safe bags.
- Remove excess air from freezer bags. (This is quite fun for my daughter.)
- Place food in the freezer.
- Make blueberry sauce from your frozen blueberries (see page 160).

Dehydrating

- Place food in the dehydrator trays or on the oven sheet.
- Place trays in the dehydrator or sheets in the oven.
- Learn to check for progress.
- Learn to turn the food.

THE BEST TOMATO, GARLIC, AND BASIL SAUCE

Friend, this sauce is one of my absolute favorites to can each summer. I love eating it with pasta in the middle of winter, and, if it is your first time canning, it is easy as well. When it comes to preserving, tomato sauce is at the top of my list. I do believe the kind of tomato you use can make for a yummier sauce. I recommend Amish Paste, San Marzano, or Martino's Roma for flavor and consistency.

NOTE: THIS RECIPE DOES NOT CONTAIN SALT BECAUSE IT WOULD CHANGE THE SAUCE'S CONSISTENCY. IT'S ALWAYS BEST TO FOLLOW A CANNING RECIPE EXACTLY. SALT AND EXTRA SEASONINGS CAN BE ADDED AFTER YOU'VE OPENED THE CANNED JAR FOR USE. ONLY AFTER OPENING SHOULD YOU ADD ADDITIONAL HERBS.

YOU WILL NEED

Standard canning supplies (see page 134)

(7) 1-pint (16-ounce [473 ml]) glass canning jars with lids and bands

20 pounds (9 kg) tomatoes (about 60 medium)

1 cup (160 g) chopped onion (I like yellow onion)

10 cloves garlic, minced

1 tablespoon (15 ml) olive oil

Fine-mesh strainer

¼ cup (5 g) finely chopped fresh basil or 1½ tablespoons (6 g) dried basil

1 tablespoon (4 g) dried oregano

1 tablespoon (15 ml) bottled lemon juice per jar

Yield: (7) 1-pint (16-ounce [473 ml]) jars or (3) 1-quart (32-ounce [946 ml]) jars

Instructions

Prepare your canning materials as directed in the first three steps of Basic Canning Steps on page 135. There's no need to start warming the jars until the sauce is almost ready.

Wash your tomatoes and remove the core and the blossom end. Quarter the tomatoes and set them aside.

Sauté the onion and garlic in the olive oil in a large pot over medium heat until translucent.

Add the tomatoes and bring to a boil.

Reduce the heat and simmer for 20 minutes, stirring occasionally.

Carefully transfer the mixture to a blender or food processor and blend until smooth, working in batches, if necessary. Strain out any seeds or peel.

Combine the strained tomato purée with the basil and oregano in the same large pot and bring it to a boil. Reduce the heat and simmer until the volume is reduced by half (about 20 minutes or so). Stir frequently to prevent burning. The color will darken and the mixture will noticeably thicken over the course of this simmer.

With the jar lifter, remove a hot jar from the canner and add 1 tablespoon (15 ml) of bottled lemon juice. Ladle the hot tomato sauce into the jar, leaving a ½ inch (1.3 cm) headspace. Remove any air bubbles with the bubble-removing tool.

Wipe the rim with a clean cloth and center the lid on the jar. Apply the band and adjust it to fingertip tight.

Use the jar lifter to place the jar back in the simmering water of the canner. Repeat the process until you've filled all the jars.

Bring the water to a boil, cover the canner, and process for 40 minutes.

Turn off the heat, remove the cover, and wait 5 minutes.

Use the jar lifter to remove the jars to a towel or cutting board.

Let them cool undisturbed.

Check the seal after 24 hours. The lids should not flex when pressed.

I adapted this recipe from one found at www.ballmasonjars.com.

Sauce for Months

One of your first goals in starting your new lifestyle can be stocking up on homemade products. Tomato sauce is an easy one! Begin with the goal of making enough sauce for three months. Drawing from personal experience, this can be achieved with just 12 tomato plants of a paste variety like Martino's Roma. These 12 plants yielded 35 pints (6 L) of sauce, and considering our household's weekly consumption of 3 to 4 pints (1.5 to 2 L), it provided enough sauce for a quarter of the year without needing to rely on store-bought alternatives.

CRUNCHY DILL PICKLES

Cucumbers are so prolific that even first-time growers often end up with an abundance. Making pickles is a great way to preserve them. I like to grow Boston and Chicago pickling cucumbers for this recipe. There is nothing like a crunchy pickle to remind you of summer's bounty, and this is a favorite to make together as a family in my house. These pickles achieve the best flavor in 3 to 6 weeks. To get them extra crunchy, place your cucumbers on ice for about 4 hours prior to canning them.

YOU WILL NEED

Standard canning supplies (see page 134)

(6) 1-pint (16-ounce [473 ml]) glass canning jars with lids and bands

2½ cups (500 g) sugar

2 tablespoons (30 g) salt

6 cups (1.4 L) apple cider vinegar

2 tablespoons (15 g) pickling spice (see sidebar)

4 pounds (1.8 kg) pickling cucumbers (about 16 small to medium)

6 heads fresh dill (about 1 per jar) or ¾ teaspoon dried dill per jar

6 cloves garlic, peeled

Yield: (6) 1-pint (16-ounce [473 ml]) jars

Instructions

Prepare your canning materials as directed in the first three steps of Basic Canning Steps on page 135. Do not bring the water to a boil.

Combine the sugar, salt, and vinegar in a large saucepan.

Tie the pickling spices in a muslin spice bag and add them to the vinegar mixture. Bring to a boil.

Reduce the heat and simmer for 15 minutes. Keep the brine hot until ready for use.

Wash and cut the cucumbers into ¼-inch (6 mm) thick slices.

With the jar lifter, remove a warm jar from the water bath canner.

Place 1 head of dill and 2 cloves garlic into the jar and pack in the cucumber slices, leaving a ½-inch (1.3 cm) headspace.

Remove the spice bag from the brine and ladle the hot liquid over the cucumbers, again leaving a ½-inch (1.3 cm) headspace.

Remove any air bubbles with the bubble-removing tool.

Wipe the rim with a clean cloth and center the lid on the jar. Apply the band and adjust it to fingertip tight.

Place the lidded jar in the canner with the jar lifter and repeat until you fill all the jars.

Bring the water to a boil, cover the pot, and process the jars for 15 minutes.

Turn off the heat and remove the lid. Wait 5 minutes.

Use the jar lifter to remove the jars and set them on a towel or cutting board.

Let them cool undisturbed.

Check the seal after 24 hours. The lids should not flex when pressed.

I adapted this recipe from one found at www.ballmasonjars.com.

My Pickling Spice Mix

YOU WILL NEED

2 tablespoons (10 g) black peppercorns

2 tablespoons (22 g) mustard seeds

2 tablespoons (10 g) coriander seeds

2 tablespoons (13 g) dill seed

1 tablespoon (6 g) allspice berries

1 teaspoon red pepper flakes

10 dried bay leaves

Instructions

Mix all the ingredients in an airtight container. This will keep for up to a year.

MY FAVORITE SALSA

There is nothing quite like a zesty homemade salsa. Made with cumin, cilantro, and oregano, this is the perfect canning recipe to gift to someone and impress your friends with all that delicious flavor. I love this recipe because it requires no peeling or prepping of the tomatoes. Easy and delicious is the way to go.

NOTE: HOMEMADE SALSA TENDS TO BE A BIT RUNNIER THAN THE STORE-BOUGHT KIND. FOR A CHUNKIER VERSION, DRAIN THE EXCESS JUICE BEFORE CANNING. THAT JUICE HAS LOTS OF FLAVOR, SO KEEP IT TO ADD TO STEWS, SOUPS, OR SALAD DRESSINGS.

YOU WILL NEED

Standard canning supplies (see page 134)

8 half-pint (8-ounce [236 ml]) glass canning jars with lids and bands

1½ cups (240 g) chopped onion (I prefer a mix of white and yellow)

2 tablespoons (20 g) chopped garlic

1 cup (236 ml) apple cider vinegar

10 cups (1.4 kg) cored, seeded, and chopped plum-type tomatoes

2 cups (260 g) seeded and chopped red and green bell peppers

1 cup (20 g) fresh cilantro (you can also use parsley)

2 tablespoons (8 g) dried oregano

1 tablespoon (12 g) sugar

2 tablespoons (30 ml) hot pepper sauce, your choice

1½ teaspoons ground cumin

1½ teaspoons salt

Yield: Approximately 8 half-pint (8-ounce [236 ml]) jars

Instructions

Prepare your canning materials as directed in the first three steps of Basic Canning Steps on page 135. Do not bring to a boil.

Combine the onions, garlic, and vinegar in a large pot and bring it to a boil.

Stir in the tomatoes and peppers and return the mixture to a boil. Cook for 3 minutes.

Add the cilantro, oregano, sugar, hot pepper sauce, cumin, and salt.

Return to a full boil, stirring constantly.

Reduce the heat and boil gently until the peppers are tender, 3 to 5 minutes.

Remove from the heat.

With the jar lifter, remove a warm jar from the water bath canner.

Ladle hot salsa into the jar, leaving a ½-inch (1 cm) headspace.

Wipe the rim with a clean cloth and center the lid on the jar. Apply the band and adjust it to fingertip tight.

Place the jar in the canner and repeat until you fill all the jars.

Bring the water to a boil, cover the canner, and process the jars for 15 minutes.

Turn off the heat and remove the cover. Wait 5 minutes.

Use the jar lifter to remove the jars and set them on a towel or cutting board.

Let them cool undisturbed.

Check the seal after 24 hours. The lids should not flex when pressed.

I adapted this recipe from one found at www.ballmasonjars.com.

LEMON MAPLE BLUEBERRY SAUCE

Every Friday night, it's a tradition in my house to have breakfast for dinner. I usually make waffles, and this sauce is the perfect accompaniment (see page 188). It's great for pancakes, too! It's quick to make with frozen blueberries, and the hints of lemon and maple balance acid and sweet. I hope this recipe becomes a tradition in your home, as well.

YOU WILL NEED

3 cups (450 g) frozen blueberries

¼ cup (60 ml) water

Juice and zest of 1 lemon

¼ cup (60 ml) maple syrup

1½ tablespoons (12 g) cornstarch dissolved in 3 tablespoons (45 ml) water

Yield: Enough for 4 large waffles

Instructions

Place the blueberries in a small saucepan. Add the water, lemon juice, zest, and maple syrup.

Turn the heat to medium and cook until the mixture comes to a low boil and the blueberries just start to break apart.

Add the dissolved cornstarch and bring the mixture to a rolling boil. Turn the heat down to a simmer and whisk for 2 to 3 minutes.

If the mixture is too thick, add a little water, 1 tablespoon (15 ml) at a time, until you reach your desired consistency.

Remove from the heat and serve warm.

MASTERING *the* HOME KITCHEN

Perhaps the best way to experience simple living is in the kitchen. In today's fast-paced world, where screens often dominate our interactions, cooking together provides a much-needed opportunity to unplug, connect on a deeper level, and be present in the moment. It's a chance to slow down and engage in an experience of the senses that fills our hearts and souls. It's also much more than just preparing a meal; it's a powerful way to connect, create memories, and foster meaningful relationships. When we cook together, we not only share the physical task of chopping, stirring, and seasoning, but we also share stories, laughter, and experiences. It's a time to bond with loved ones. This must be why the kitchen is often referred to as the heart of the home. Some of my fondest memories are of being in the kitchen with my grandma. Born and raised in Cuba, she made the best black beans you've ever tasted. The kitchen was her workroom, and she loved serving others food from the heart.

I wrote this chapter to encourage you to make more home-cooked meals. Learn to make foods from scratch and feel the benefits it brings. When I first moved to the country, I thought I cooked at home pretty frequently. However, I quickly realized how often I had been going out for lunch and dinner. With the nearest grocery store no longer a mere five-minute drive away, I knew something had to change. Suddenly having to cook two or three meals a day was a significant adjustment, and it took some time to get used to it. Eventually, making homemade meals became part of my daily routine and it's something I take great pride in. I want to encourage you to do the same.

SEASONAL EATING

Once I started cooking more meals at home, I wanted to ensure I was taking every measure possible to provide my family with the most nutrient-dense food. This led me to research how seasonal eating is so beneficial to our bodies. Seasonal eating is not a recent health trend but a practice passed down through generations, in part because, for a long time, the only choice was to eat what was in season or what you could preserve: asparagus in spring, watermelon in summer, pears in fall, citrus fruits in winter. Now, many of us have access to whatever foods we want at any time of year.

Returning to seasonal eating takes changing one's mindset, especially when planning meals, but I promise you it is possible and will be much better for you. Eating seasonally means indulging in fruits and vegetables when they are ripe in your specific area, town, or country.

The benefits of seasonal eating are numerous. Not only are these foods tastier, fresher, and more nutritious but they are also harvested and consumed at their peak ripeness. The quicker they are enjoyed, the better! Unlike out-of-season produce that is often picked prematurely and travels long distances to reach store shelves, seasonal produce does not require excessive use of pesticides, preservatives, or waxes. With minimal human intervention, they rely on the region's weather and natural growing conditions.

Growing your vegetables can be the most cost-effective option in the long run; however, buying in-season produce can still be more affordable as it is abundantly available. Locally sourced fruits and vegetables do not require extensive storage or expensive transportation, resulting in more cost savings. I love to purchase extra seasonal produce to preserve for later use—such as gathering extra blueberries to freeze and use later for blueberry sauce (see page 160).

Buying locally grown seasonal produce also promotes sustainable living for farmers and invests in your community. I believe it's so important to support local agriculture. Plan to visit your local farmers' market once a month and stock up on some seasonal produce. By supporting local agriculture you'll also reduce your carbon footprint and help foster a more sustainable and resilient food system.

Why Cook Homemade Meals

Moving to the country shifted my mindset. As a former ICU nurse, I came face-to-face with death and the harsh reality of the many diseases we face. Living a healthy lifestyle is incredibly important and what you eat is a key part of that. Making meals at home is one way to take ownership of your health. Knowing that I am providing my family with delicious, nutrient-dense food brings me joy. Although the taste of homemade food may be different without the fillers and added flavors found in store-bought food, it is much more satisfying and life-giving. With time, you will adjust to the fresh taste and crave all the delicious goodness homemade meals bring.

Next time you go to the grocery store, take a moment to look at the food labels. Do you recognize all the ingredients? Are there some things you can make from scratch instead of purchasing them at the store? Cook dry beans instead of buying canned, boil potatoes and mash them instead of purchasing potato flakes. Don't do it all in one day, but make small steps toward actionable change. Plan one night a week where you cook a meal from scratch and eat dinner together as a family. Once it becomes a part of your routine, add another night, and so forth. Learn to make some of the staples and seasonings you use every day. You will not only feel better, but you'll also feel fuller and more satisfied after your meals than ever before.

Seasons for Food

Here are a few ideas on foods that might be in season depending on the time of year. There will be variables depending on where you live.

Use these lists as a general guide when shopping and meal planning.

Spring	Summer	Fall	Winter
Apricots	Apples	Apples	Apples
Artichokes	Apricots	Bananas	Arugula
Arugula	Basil	Beets	Avocados
Asparagus	Beets	Bell peppers	Bananas
Broccoli	Bell peppers	Brussels sprouts	Beets
Carrots	Blackberries	Cabbage	Brussels sprouts
Cauliflower	Blueberries	Carrots	Cabbage
Celery	Cantaloupe	Cauliflower	Carrots
Chives	Carrots	Collard greens	Citrus (grapefruit,
Collard greens	Celery	Garlic	lemons, limes,
Lemons	Cherries	Ginger	oranges)
Lettuce	Corn	Green beans	Collard greens
Mushrooms	Cucumbers	Kiwifruit	Kale
Peas	Eggplant	Lemons	Leeks
Pineapple	Garlic	Lettuce	Onions
Radishes	Honeydew melon	Mushrooms	Pears
Rhubarb	Jalapeños	Onions	Pomegranates
Spinach	Nasturtium	Parsnips	Potatoes
Spring onions	Okra	Pears	Pumpkins
(scallions)	Peaches	Peas	Spinach
Strawberries	Plums	Pineapple	Turnips
Turnips	Raspberries	Potatoes	Winter squash
	Summer squash	Pumpkin	
	Tomatillos	Radishes	
	Tomatoes	Spinach	
	Watermelon	Sweet potatoes	
	Zucchini	Swiss chard	
		Turnips	
		Winter squash	

Planning Seasonal Meals

Shifting my mindset to eating more within the seasons has significantly impacted my meal planning. Instead of focusing on my food preferences, I plan meals around what's in season or growing in my garden. It's all about asking yourself what's available and what makes sense to eat. For instance, during warm weather, I crave more salads and grilled veggies, while in the colder months, I opt for hearty soups with winter squash. My body tends to crave seasonal items naturally and I've found that incorporating them into my meals has been both delicious and nutritious.

While I somewhat plan what I'll cook during the week, I don't tend to be too rigid or detailed. Cooking on a whim and using what I have on hand allows for more creativity in the kitchen, especially when cooking from scratch. If you prefer a specific plan, that's fine, too, if you follow some general guidelines.

Having some ingredients prepped and ready in the fridge—for example, chopped peppers and onions to add to a stir-fry or fajitas—can make cooking a breeze. When roasting vegetables in the oven, throw in a few extra items, like sweet potatoes or potatoes, that you can use throughout the week. During the fall and winter, I keep staples, such as cabbage, broccoli, citrus, and squash, in the fridge; during spring, I load up on greens. In the summer, I freeze produce, such as corn and peppers, to use in recipes later, and frozen fruit is perfect for whipping up delicious smoothies for breakfast.

You can create delicious, nutrient-dense food by experimenting in the kitchen with simple ingredients. To add extra flavor to most meals, I add fresh seasonal herbs. Oatmeal is a household staple and the perfect base for adding seasonal fruits. You don't need a specific recipe for this; just toss in some blueberries during the summer or crunchy apples in the fall. Make a list of what your family loves to eat and find ways to incorporate some seasonal produce into those meals. Have fun in the kitchen. Experiment. Some of my best recipes happened when I just made it up with what I had on hand. Here's a little tip, though: make sure you write it down, so you remember how to make it again.

SPRING VEGETABLE POT PIE

There's nothing quite so comforting as a warm, delicious pot pie. This vegan one is simple to make with seasonal ingredients you have on hand. Serve it right out of the cast-iron skillet and be prepared to make it repeatedly. Use squash, bell peppers, and corn for summer and butternut squash, cauliflower, and carrots in the fall. Or get creative. Either way, enjoy every delicious bite.

YOU WILL NEED

1 pound (454 g) Yukon gold potatoes, cut into bite-size chunks

2 cups (240 g) chopped carrots (cut into half-moons)

3 tablespoons (45 ml) olive oil or plant-based butter, plus more for the crust

1 onion or leek, finely chopped

4 cloves garlic, finely chopped

1 bulb fennel (quartered, then cut into desired size)

1 cup (120 g) chopped asparagus, (cut into ½-inch [1 cm] pieces)

1 cup (236 ml) vegetable broth

1 cup (236 ml) full-fat coconut milk

¼ cup (30 g) cornstarch

1 cup (150 g) frozen peas

Juice of 1½ lemons

Zest of 1 lemon

2 teaspoons (10 g) Dijon mustard

½ teaspoon sea salt

1 teaspoon garlic powder

1 teaspoon onion powder

1 tablespoon (4 g) fresh thyme, lemon or regular

1 tablespoon (4 g) fresh tarragon

2 tablespoons (5 g) fresh chives

1 package plant-based puff pastry dough*

Yield: 6 servings

Instructions

Preheat the oven to 425°F (232°C).

Fill a large pot with enough salted water to cover the potatoes and carrots. Bring it to a boil, then reduce the heat.

Add the potatoes and carrots. Simmer for 10 minutes or until fork tender. Drain and set aside.

In a 10-inch (25 cm) cast-iron or oven-safe skillet, heat the olive oil and sauté the onion, garlic, and fennel until translucent. (You can also use a regular pan and transfer the filling to an oven-safe dish.)

Add the asparagus and sauté a few minutes longer.

Add the carrots, potatoes, and vegetable broth. Mix well.

Make a space in the middle of the pan and add the coconut milk.

Whisk in the cornstarch until it dissolves, then mix everything well.

Add the peas, lemon juice, zest, mustard, sea salt, garlic powder, thyme, tarragon, and chives.

Mix well and adjust the seasonings to your taste.

Remove it from the heat and allow the filling to cool.

Continued

Roll out the pastry dough to ⅛ inch (3 mm) thick and cut it into the shape of your pan.

Place the pastry to cover the whole pan. The dough will shrink as it bakes, so overlap is okay.

Score the pastry with a sharp knife and brush the top with olive oil.

Place the pan in the oven and cook for 20 minutes.

Lower the heat to 375°F (191°C) and cook for another 10 to 15 minutes or until the crust is puffy and golden.

Cool slightly before serving.

NOTE: STRETCH YOUR INGREDIENTS AND BRING MORE SEASONAL GOODNESS TO YOUR MEALS BY USING LEFTOVER CARROT TOPS FOR PESTO, LEEK PARTS FOR VEGETABLE BROTH (SEE PAGE 184), AND FENNEL FRONDS IN SALAD.

Substitute pie crust, if desired (see page 190).

SUMMER WATERMELON SALAD WITH HONEY-LIME DRESSING AND FRESH HERBS

One of the benefits of eating seasonally is the hydration you get from fresh summer fruit. I love juicy watermelons on a hot day. I make this salad on repeat over the season, especially for summer gatherings.

YOU WILL NEED

1 small watermelon, seeded and cubed (approximately 3 cups [600 g])

2 tablespoons (30 g) honey

Zest and juice of 1 lime

5 fresh basil leaves

5 fresh mint leaves

Salt, to taste

Yield: 4 servings

Instructions

Put the watermelon in a medium bowl.

Drizzle with the honey and toss gently.

Zest the lime over the salad, then squeeze in the juice. Watch out for seeds!

Chiffonade the basil and mint leaves, then add them to the salad.

Toss again and sprinkle with salt, as desired.

Serve chilled.

NOTE: HONEY AND LIME PAIR BEAUTIFULLY WITH ANY FRUIT SALAD. USE IT OVER PINEAPPLE AND STRAWBERRIES IN THE SPRING OR ORANGE WEDGES IN THE WINTER. TRY OTHER VARIATIONS TO FIND YOUR PERFECT COMBINATION.

FALL ARUGULA AND SPINACH SALAD WITH APPLES, SALTED ALMONDS, AND DRIED FIGS

Salad is one of my favorite ways to eat all the delicious seasonal produce fall brings. You can make this one with any greens you have on hand. I love spinach and arugula, but kale is a tasty alternative. The dressing is my number one go-to recipe for almost any salad. I promise it will be a hit for the whole family. I usually make a double recipe to keep and use throughout the week. It stores well in the fridge for up to 10 days.

YOU WILL NEED

For the Dressing:

¼ cup (60 ml) olive oil

2 tablespoons (30 ml) maple syrup

1 teaspoon Dijon mustard

1 teaspoon apple cider vinegar

3 cloves garlic, crushed

1 teaspoon dried oregano or 1 tablespoon (4 g) fresh, very finely chopped

Salt, to taste

Pinch of red pepper flakes, optional

For the Salad:

3 cups (60 g) arugula

3 cups (60 g) spinach

2 crunchy apples, such as Fuji or Granny Smith, washed and thinly sliced

10 to 12 dried or fresh figs, halved

8 ounces (227 g) feta cheese (I use plant-based)

½ cup (75 g) salted sliced almonds

½ red onion, thinly sliced

Yield: 6 servings

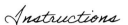

Instructions

To make the dressing: Add the dressing ingredients to a small jar, close it tightly, and shake to combine.

To make the salad: Put the arugula and spinach in a large bowl, then add the apples and figs. Top with the feta, almonds, and red onion.

Pour the dressing over the salad and toss gently.

Serve immediately.

NOTE: YOU CAN MAKE THIS SALAD WITH WHATEVER SEASONAL PRODUCE IS AVAILABLE. IN THE SUMMER, USE ROMAINE AND TOMATOES; CONSIDER KALE AND PEAR IN THE WINTER. USE TOASTED PECANS INSTEAD OF ALMONDS. THE OPTIONS ARE ENDLESS.

WINTER BAKED PEARS WITH HONEY, PECANS, AND CRANBERRIES

Baked fruit is the perfect excuse to satisfy a sweet tooth without too much guilt. Drizzled with honey, vanilla, nutmeg, and pecan topping and served with cranberries and ice cream, this makes a super easy and yummy dessert. You can also serve it for breakfast. Use whichever variety of pear you prefer, but Bosc pears retain their flavor, shape, and texture when baked, cooked, or poached. This recipe also works well for apples!

YOU WILL NEED

3 Bosc pears, halved and cored

½ cup (118 g) honey, divided

1 teaspoon vanilla extract

1 teaspoon ground cinnamon

Pinch of nutmeg

½ cup (75 g) pecans, chopped

10 to 12 fresh cranberries

Yield: 6 servings

Instructions

Preheat the oven to 350°F (177°C).

Remove a sliver off the back of each pear to allow it to lie flat.

Place the pears, cut-side up, in a glass or ceramic 9 × 13-inch (23 × 33 cm) baking dish. They should look like little boats.

Combine half of the honey with the vanilla, cinnamon, nutmeg, and pecans.

Drizzle the other half of the honey over the pears.

Add some of the pecan mixture to the inside of each pear.

Add one cranberry to each pear and put the rest in the baking dish for color.

Bake for 25 to 30 minutes or until the pears are golden and as soft as you'd like.

Serve with ice cream or enjoy as is!

KITCHEN & PANTRY ESSENTIALS

––––––

A kitchen with clean countertops and everything put away might look pretty, but a working kitchen with everything you need is helpful. I realized I had to make my kitchen into a place where I *wanted* to cook. I have all my basic cooking essentials at hand and ready to use. I keep cast-iron pans on my stove, a vintage crock holds wooden spoons, salt is in a jar for easy sprinkling, dishes and glasses are on open shelves—you get the idea. It makes all the difference and saves me so much time. My kitchen drawers are not perfectly organized, but I can easily reach for measuring cups and mixing bowls. Go through your kitchen and get rid of what you don't use or need. Less is more. When you declutter, it helps you be more intentional, and you will find true joy in the kitchen.

A well-stocked pantry is essential for learning to cook from scratch. It will help you make meals and remove some stress when planning. You can create an entire meal without going to the grocery store. I love keeping 5-gallon (19 kg) food-grade buckets filled with the dry foods we always

eat, such as rice, lentils, flour, and oats. I order these items in bulk and always have about a six month's supply available. Yes, they take up space, but having them on hand means I can quickly grab what I need without worrying about going to the store. So, I converted a coat closet into an extra pantry. Yes, it means I have less storage for clothes, but having healthy food available when needed makes all the difference. Do what works for you, your family, and the space you have. Then, learn the art of turning simple pantry ingredients into meals.

My Kitchen Must-Haves

I use a variety of items in the kitchen, but I tend to reach for some more often than others. Identify the items you use frequently and keep them within easy reach. This way, you can quickly grab what you need without searching cabinets or drawers. Here are a few of my most frequently used items.

Cookware and Utensils

Cast-iron cookware

Citrus juicer

Dutch oven

Glass baking dishes

Glass mixing bowls

Kitchen scale

Kitchen shears

Measuring cups and spoons

Set of good kitchen knives

Vegetable peeler

Wood cutting board

Wooden spoons

Pantry Staples

All-purpose flour

Almond butter

Apple cider vinegar

Brown rice

Canned jalapeños

Canned salsa

Chocolate chips

Coarse sea salt

Coconut oil

Cornstarch

Dried beans
(black beans,
garbanzos, etc.)

Dried fruit
(apples, apricots,
raisins, etc.)

Fine sea salt

Gluten-free oats

Lentils

Maple syrup

Nuts (almonds,
cashews, peanuts,
pecans, etc.)

Olive oil

Organic whole cane
sugar

Pasta

Peanut butter

Raw honey

Tomato sauce

Vanilla extract

White rice

White vinegar

How to Clean and Care for Cast-Iron Pans

Cast iron is my absolute favorite vessel to cook in. It is durable, versatile, and a reliable cooking material with excellent heat retention properties. I can use it on stovetops, in ovens, or over an open flame and it is perfect for both savory and sweet dishes. My favorite things to cook in cast iron are pancakes and cinnamon rolls, sautéed veggies, stir-fry, fried potatoes, pot pie, and cobblers. I use stainless steel pots only for steaming veggies or cooking soups and stews. Cast iron is indestructible and will last you a lifetime—in fact, you can pass it down through the generations.

Caring for cast iron is a little more involved than for most other types of cookware, but it is very manageable. The key is seasoning, or creating and maintaining a nonstick surface that protects the cast iron, helps prevent rust, and is longer-lasting and healthier for you than manufactured nonstick coatings. Oil heated on the cast-iron surface bonds with the metal to form a protective layer. With continued use, the layer becomes thicker and the surface becomes more nonstick, making it easier to cook with and clean.

Continued

There are differing opinions on how to clean and care for cast iron, but here is what has worked for me.

To season it:

1) Preheat your oven to 450°F (232°C).

2) Scrub unseasoned cast iron or cast iron with broken-down seasoning with hot soapy water. Use a stainless steel or chainmail scrubber to remove any debris.

3) Dry well with a towel.

4) Lightly coat every part of the cast iron, including the handle and bottom, with coconut oil or other oil with a high smoke point, such as flax or avocado. Do not use olive oil.

5) Wipe away any excess oil that might cause the cast iron to smoke.

6) Place the cast iron upside down in the oven for about an hour, then turn off the oven and let the cast iron cool completely before removing it.

7) If it has a shiny black luster and isn't tacky to the touch, it is ready.

NOTE: EXPERTS RECOMMEND OILING CAST IRON AFTER EVERY USE. I JUST RUB A LITTLE BIT OF COCONUT OIL ON THE PANS EACH TIME. YOU CAN SEASON IT TWO OR THREE TIMES A YEAR, OR AS NEEDED.

To clean it:

1) Use a wooden spatula to remove any food debris.

2) Clean the cast iron with warm water and a stainless steel or chainmail scrubber to remove any remaining debris, if necessary.

3) It is not recommended to use soap, as doing so might strip the cast iron of its seasoning. However, I sometimes do use soap with warm water to help soften stuck-on food. If you use it, be sure to rinse thoroughly and check that the seasoning is still intact.

Tips for cooking with it:

- Always preheat the skillet before adding anything to cast iron, even oil.

- Add a little bit of oil or butter to the pan before you put anything else in it.

- Try not to flip and mix a lot when warming food. (I have found that the more you move things around, the more it coats the pan with other substances and can tend to stick.)

Essential Seasoning Recipes

Making homemade spice mixes instead of using store-bought ones has many benefits, including that they are a lot fresher and more flavorful than the ones at the store. Plus, many store-bought seasonings, such as Italian or taco seasoning, contain additives and preservatives. Making your own can also be cost-effective, as you can buy bulk spices and create more significant quantities of the mix at a lower cost per serving. My goal has been to decrease the need for the grocery store and make more of my own things, so creating spice blends is quite fun and helps me add flavor to meals.

HOMEMADE ITALIAN SEASONING

3 tablespoons (12 g) dried basil

3 tablespoons (12 g) dried oregano

2 tablespoons (8 g) dried parsley

1 tablespoon (4 g) dried sage

1 tablespoon (4 g) dried thyme

1½ tablespoons (9 g) garlic powder

2 teaspoons (4 g) onion powder

1 teaspoon dried rosemary

½ teaspoon red pepper flakes

¼ teaspoon black pepper

Instructions

Combine all the ingredients and store them in an airtight container for up to a year.

HOMEMADE TACO SEASONING

3 tablespoons (24 g) chili powder

1½ tablespoons (9 g) ground cumin

1 tablespoon (6 g) garlic powder

1 tablespoon (6 g) paprika

2 teaspoons (4 g) onion powder

1½ teaspoons dried oregano

1½ teaspoons sea salt

¾ teaspoon black pepper

Instructions

Combine all the ingredients and store them in an airtight container for up to a year.

HOMEMADE SEASONED SALT

½ cup (118 g) salt

1 tablespoon (12 g) sugar

1 teaspoon garlic powder

1 teaspoon onion powder

1 tablespoon (6 g) paprika

½ teaspoon celery seed

½ teaspoon black pepper

Instructions

Combine all the ingredients and store them in an airtight container for up to a year.

HOMEMADE CHILI SEASONING

¼ cup (32 g) chili powder

¼ cup (24 g) cumin

¼ cup (24 g) smoked paprika

2 teaspoons (3 g) dried oregano

1 tablespoon (6 g) garlic powder

1 tablespoon (6 g) onion powder

1 teaspoon sea salt

1 teaspoon red pepper flakes, or to taste

Instructions

Combine all the ingredients and store them in an airtight container for up to a year.

HOMEMADE RANCH SEASONING

¼ cup (24 g) onion powder

1 tablespoon (6 g) celery salt

2 tablespoons (8 g) dried parsley flakes

1 tablespoon (10 g) poppy seeds

1 tablespoon (3 g) dill weed

2 teaspoons (4 g) garlic powder

2 teaspoons (3 g) dried basil

1½ teaspoons salt

Instructions

Combine all the ingredients and store them in an airtight container for up to a year.

HOMEMADE HERBES DE PROVENCE SEASONING

2 tablespoons (8 g) dried basil

2 tablespoons (8 g) dried thyme

2 tablespoons (8 g) dried oregano

2 tablespoons (8 g) dried savory

2 tablespoons (8 g) dried marjoram

2 tablespoons (8 g) dried rosemary

2 tablespoons (16 g) fennel seeds

1 tablespoon (3 g) dried lavender

Instructions

Combine all the ingredients and store them in an airtight container for up to a year.

RANCH DRESSING MADE WITH HOMEMADE SEASONING

1 cup (236 g) mayonnaise

2 tablespoons (30 ml) lemon juice (or more if desired)

¼ cup (60 ml) water

1 heaping tablespoon (10 g) homemade ranch seasoning mix (see top left)

Instructions

Whisk together the mayonnaise, lemon juice, and water. Add the ranch seasoning and mix well. Enjoy!

HOMEMADE VEGETABLE BROTH

Making homemade broth used to intimidate me. I felt it was complicated and time-consuming. As it turns out, it is one of the simplest ways to infuse meals with flavor. Here's how I make what I call zero-waste broth.

The first step is to accumulate and freeze your veggie scraps: peels, trimmings, tops, ends from carrots, onions, peppers, celery, tomatoes, and so on—anything you didn't use the first time around. I usually have enough in two weeks to make a few jars of broth.

YOU WILL NEED

Vegetable scraps

Fresh herbs of choice (thyme, oregano, and bay leaves work well)

1 onion, chopped*

1 head garlic, divided into cloves*

Water (amount varies)

Salt

 Instructions

In a large pot, combine the veggie scraps, herbs, and onion and garlic, if using.

Add just enough water for the vegetables to start floating. Too much water makes a weak broth. I use about 1 gallon (3.8 L) of water for 1½ gallons (5.7 L) of frozen scraps, plus the small amount of fresh herbs and vegetables.

Add salt to taste. You can adjust this later.

Bring to a boil and then reduce to a simmer. Cover the pot in such a way that a bit of steam can escape.

Simmer for 45 to 60 minutes, then test the flavor. If the broth is too bitter, consider adding more carrots, bell peppers, or tomatoes.

Pour the broth through a strainer. Compost the solids or feed them to your chickens, if you have them.

Freeze your broth in freezer-safe jars or bags or other freezer-safe containers for up to 6 months.

The additional onion and garlic are optional. If you feel you have enough of each in your scraps, you can omit them.

CRUNCHY HOMEMADE GRANOLA

This is one of the easiest ways to replace a store-bought item. Not only does homemade granola have much less sugar than what you find at the store, but it's also so much crunchier and tastier. You can add in whatever you want, including some of the ingredients you've preserved, such as dried figs and dehydrated strawberries! I make a large batch twice a month to use as a quick and healthy breakfast for the family. You can give it as a gift, too! Use the suggested variations with the base recipe or make up your own combination.

YOU WILL NEED

Base Granola Recipe:

4½ cups (360 g) rolled oats (I use gluten-free)

1½ teaspoons ground cinnamon

½ teaspoon salt

¾ cup (177 ml) pure maple syrup (up to 1 cup [236 ml] if a sweeter granola is desired)

½ cup (118 ml) melted coconut oil

2 tablespoons (30 ml) vanilla extract

Yield: 8 servings

Instructions

Preheat the oven to 300°F (150°C) and cover one or two rimmed baking sheets with parchment paper (I do one recipe on two baking sheets).

In a large bowl, combine the oats, cinnamon, and salt. Set aside.

In a medium bowl or large measuring cup, combine the maple syrup, coconut oil, and vanilla.

Mix the liquid ingredients into the dry ingredients, stirring or tossing until the oats are well coated.

Spread the granola evenly over the prepared baking sheets.

Bake for 45 minutes, turning every 15 minutes.

Let it cool completely before storing it in an airtight container for up to 1 month.

Variations

Apple Cranberry Granola: Add dried apple chips, dried cranberries, and sliced almonds.

Orange & Almond Granola: Add toasted almonds, orange zest, and golden raisins.

Chocolate Pecan Granola: Add chocolate chips and pecans.

Tropical Granola: Add dried pineapple, chia seeds, and coconut flakes.

THE PERFECT BREAKFAST WAFFLES

Every Friday evening, we sit down as a family and have breakfast for dinner. It has become a tradition and something I look forward to every week. These waffles are my absolute favorite and contain healthy ingredients—all of which I keep stocked in my pantry.

YOU WILL NEED

2 cups (240 g) all-purpose flour (substitute gluten-free at a ratio of 1:1)

2 tablespoons (16 g) baking powder

1 teaspoon sea salt

(1) 15-ounce (425 g) can full-fat coconut milk

¼ cup (60 ml) water

2 tablespoons (30 ml) maple syrup or honey

1 ripe banana, smashed, optional

Yield: 4 to 6 servings

Instructions

Whisk together the flour, baking powder, and sea salt in a large bowl.

Add the coconut milk, water, and maple syrup. Mix well.

Add the bananas, if desired.

If the batter is too thick, add 1 tablespoon (15 ml) of water at a time until you get the right consistency.

Heat a waffle maker to medium-high and coat the plates with a little butter.

Pour ¼ to ½ cup (60 to 118 g) of batter onto the waffle maker.

Cook for about 5 minutes or until ready.

Serve warm. Leftovers freeze well and you can reheat them in the toaster.

NOTE: FEEL FREE TO DRESS UP THESE WAFFLES BY ADDING 1 TABLESPOON (15 ML) VANILLA, ALMOND, OR LEMON EXTRACT; MIXING IN SOME CHOCOLATE CHIPS OR PECANS OR SERVING WITH FRESH FRUIT, HOMEMADE BLUEBERRY SAUCE (SEE PAGE 160), OR MAPLE BUTTER (SEE BELOW).

Quick Maple Butter

YOU WILL NEED

2 sticks (8 ounces [227 g]) unsalted butter, at room temperature

¾ cup (177 ml) maple syrup

½ teaspoon salt

Instructions

In a medium bowl, mix the ingredients well. The maple butter keeps in the refrigerator for up to a month in an airtight container.

FLAKY PIE CRUST

If there were ever a perfect recipe to make together as a family in the kitchen, it has to be this pie crust. It takes a little time, but the fun you'll have and the crust you'll make are worth it. Use this recipe for pies, pastries, empanadas, crackers, quiches, and more. If you don't have a food processor, you can use a pastry blender. It will just take more time and muscle.

YOU WILL NEED

2¼ cups (270 g) unbleached all-purpose flour or a pastry flour blend

¼ teaspoon salt (omit if using salted butter)

¼ teaspoon baking powder

¾ cup (180 g) + 1 tablespoon (15 g) COLD butter (I use plant-based), cubed

1½ tablespoons (23 ml) buttermilk*

4+ tablespoons (60+ ml) COLD water

1 egg beaten with 1 tablespoon (15 ml) water, or plant-based milk as needed

Yield: (1) 9-inch (23 cm) pie crust

Instructions

Pulse the flour, salt, and baking powder in a food processor until combined.

Add the cold butter cubes and pulse until the mixture forms big crumbles. Do not over-pulse.

Add the buttermilk then add 4 tablespoons (60 ml) of water and mix until it makes a ball-like consistency. Add a bit more water (up to 2 tablespoons [30 ml]) if needed.

Remove the dough from the food processor and roll it into a ball. Cover it with plastic wrap and refrigerate it for about 30 minutes.

Roll out the dough and place it on a 9-inch (23 cm) pie dish. Let it hang over the edges.

Trim away the excess and poke holes in the bottom of the crust with a fork.

If you have time, refrigerate it for another 20 to 30 minutes before baking. This will ensure a flaky crust!

Preheat the oven to 350°F (177°C).

Brush it with egg wash or a plant-based alternative, such as almond milk.

Add filling, if using, and bake for 30 minutes. Cover the edges of the crust with a silicone shield or aluminum foil to prevent them from burning.

For other recipes, follow the cooking time on the recipe once the crust is ready for use. If you are making a pie with a cold filling, you may bake the crust as instructed, but without filling inside. Add your filling once the crust is cool.

I make my own plant-based buttermilk by adding 1 teaspoon of apple cider vinegar to 1 tablespoon (15 ml) of almond milk. Let it curdle for 10 minutes.

RUSTIC ARTISAN BREAD

Once you start baking bread, your house will smell like a bakery. You'll be surprised at how easily this recipe comes together—it takes just minutes and requires very little work. This bread has just four ingredients but you'll get a loaf that's delicious in flavor, crispy on the outside, and tender on the inside. And this bread is also much healthier than what you find at the store. Baking bread is so comforting, and I love sharing my homemade bread with friends and family. It's a great way to say "I love you."

YOU WILL NEED

3 cups (360 g) all-purpose flour, plus 1½ tablespoons (12 g), for dusting

2 teaspoons (10 g) kosher salt

1 teaspoon yeast (instant is best)

1½ cups (354 ml) warm water (not boiling)

Instructions

Combine the flour, salt, and yeast in the bowl of a stand mixer with a dough hook or use a wooden spoon and a large bowl to make the recipe by hand.

Slowly add the water and mix until combined. It will look sloppy. Do not overmix.

Cover the bowl and let the dough rise. You need to be patient, leaving it alone for anywhere from 1 to 24 hours; I recommend at least 4. The longer you allow it to sit, the more it will have a sourdough-like flavor and consistency.

Once the dough has at least doubled in size, preheat your oven to 450°F (232°C).

Generously flour your countertop and pour the sticky dough onto it.

Shape the dough into a ball and tuck any pieces sticking out down to the bottom of the ball. Do this for only about 15 seconds. If the dough is too sticky, dust it with a little more flour.

Place the ball on parchment paper and let it sit while the oven warms up.

Score the top of the bread with a sharp knife to let the steam escape.

Place the bread and the parchment paper into a Dutch oven.

Cover and bake for 30 minutes.

Uncover and bake for an additional 15 minutes.

Carefully remove the bread from the Dutch oven and set it on a cooling rack. Cover it with a lightweight flour sack or towel. The bread will soften as it cools.

NOTE: WHILE YOU CAN MAKE THIS BREAD ON A PIZZA STONE, I RECOMMEND A DUTCH OVEN. IT HELPS BAKE THE BEST BREAD AND IS THE EASIEST WAY TO MAKE IT, IN MY OPINION.

HOMEMADE PIZZA CRUST

I have found homemade pizza to be one of my favorite things to make from scratch. A delicious way to eat it is with homemade pesto and fresh garden peaches. You can also do a traditional tomato sauce with lots of garlic. I use my friend Angela's family recipe for the crust and it is so delicious every time My daughter loves to help me roll out the dough, which is so crunchy and delicious fresh out of the oven. Who doesn't love pizza?

YOU WILL NEED

⅓ cup (80 ml) water

2 tablespoons (30 ml) olive oil

1 cup (120 g) all-purpose flour, plus more for dusting

¼ teaspoon baking powder

¼ teaspoon salt

Your choice of sauce, toppings, and cheese

A few favorites toppings in our home include:
Spring: asparagus, artichoke hearts, and capers
Summer: roasted peaches with pesto
Fall: caramelized onions and fig
Winter: squash and kale

Yield: (1) 10 to 12-inch (25 to 30 cm) crust

Preheat the oven to 450°F (232°C). If you have a pizza stone, put it in now.

Combine the water, oil, flour, baking powder, and salt in a large bowl and mix them thoroughly with your hands, making a ball.

Dust your countertop with flour and put the ball of dough on it.

Roll the dough to your desired thickness. You get a crunchier crust at ¼-inch (6 mm) thick and a chewier one at ½-inch (1.2 cm) thick. I roll it thin and it bakes in about 10 minutes.

Move the crust to the pizza stone or onto a pan large enough to accommodate it. Spread with your choice of sauce, toppings, and cheese.

Bake until the crust is crisp on the bottom and the toppings are golden. Timing will depend on the thickness of the crust and the amount of sauce and toppings.

NOTE: ROLL DOUGH TO ¼ INCH (6 MM) THICK FOR A CRUNCHIER CRUST AND ½ INCH (1 CM) THICK FOR A CHEWIER CRUST. THIS RECIPE CAN BE USED TO MAKE A FLATBREAD AS WELL.

THE ROLE OF FAMILY
IN THE HOME KITCHEN

———

Making more meals from scratch means more time spent in the kitchen. This is the perfect time to make cooking a family affair. Here are some suggestions for how to make the kitchen the true heart of the home and a wonderful place to be.

- Plan your meals together as a family. Ask each person what they love to eat and consider ways to incorporate that into your meals.

- Gather ingredients together as a family. This could be harvesting items from your garden or selecting produce at the grocery store. Show kids where their food comes from and the journey from farm to their plate.

- Give each family member a specific task to do when preparing a meal. This could be washing vegetables, measuring ingredients, or stirring the pot, or it could mean setting or clearing the table and washing dishes afterward. Bring infants into the kitchen with you to let them observe you as you cook and experience the sounds, textures, smells, tastes, and sights of cooking.

- Encourage everyone to work together as a team. This will help the process move along faster and create a sense of teamwork.

- If you have created a new recipe, have older family members write it on a recipe card or book to remember for next time.

- Decorate aprons together and wear them each time you cook.

- Have fun! Play French music in the background for ambience each time you cook and have breakfast for dinner instead of a typical dinner meal.

SETTING THE DINNER TABLE

Here is a unique way to set the dinner table beautifully and involve the whole family.

YOU WILL NEED

A roll of kraft paper

Seasonal flowers

Dinner plates

Chalk markers

Instructions

Make a table runner out of the kraft paper. You can secure it, if needed.

Decorate the table with seasonal flowers.

At each place around the table, trace a dinner plate and write one person's name. If you like, personalize each circle with words or drawings—maybe the person's favorite plant, animal, or hobby. Alternatively, every day, have each family member write a word of praise or a positive phrase to describe that family member. By the end of the week, these words and pictures will fill the table just as much as the food you serve there, affirming and bonding you together.

Use this table runner for a whole week, and then make a new one, if you'd like. You can even switch up who sits where.

NOTE: POTATO STAMPS ARE ANOTHER FUN WAY TO ADD TO YOUR KRAFT PAPER RUNNER. CUT A LARGE POTATO IN HALF AND USE A COOKIE CUTTER TO CARVE OUT A SHAPE. DIP THE END INTO PAINT AND DECORATE THE KRAFT PAPER. IT'S EASY AND FUN, PLUS ANOTHER WAY TO PERSONALIZE YOUR DINNER TABLE. JUST MAKE SURE IT'S DRY BEFORE PEOPLE SIT DOWN TO EAT!

Thank you, friend, for taking the time to read this book. I poured my heart and soul into each chapter and my hope is the lessons and tips I've learned over the years can help you on your journey.

Start applying these principles without hesitation today. I promise you'll be glad you did.

ACKNOWLEDGMENTS

Writing and creating *Simple Country Living* has been a longtime dream of mine. I am nothing but grateful for the opportunity to share my heart with you. However, this book would not have been possible without the help and support of so many. It is because of all of them that this book came to fruition. A page of acknowledgments pales compared to how I feel, but this will at least thank those who have made the most significant impact throughout this book-writing journey.

To my husband, Jared. Your unwavering support and encouragement have been the cornerstone of all my life endeavors. You have been my greatest champion in this process, from watching

Ava while I poured my thoughts onto paper to being my biggest cheerleader. Your love and dedication mean everything and I am eternally grateful for the life we have created together.

To my daughter, Ava. Thank you for loving me and being my sidekick through life. Your enthusiasm and joy are infectious. Thank you for hanging by my side and encouraging me to "keep writing, Mommy." You are the reason I chase my dreams.

I extend my deepest thanks to my parents, who emigrated from Cuba in search of freedom. Your love and support have always been a constant source of comfort and inspiration. I felt your excitement for this book and I am grateful you planted the seed in me years ago to live for God and be a light for others. To my mom, who is an amazing writer, thank you for your support. And to my dad, who taught me from a very young age to love the garden, I am so grateful for the memories we have created together planting seeds.

A special thank you goes out to my dear friend Kristen, whose photography skills brought this book to life. Your keen eye for beauty and attention to detail allowed us to capture the essence of a simple country life in a way that I know will inspire my readers. Your countless hours spent behind the lens and in the editing room have not gone unnoticed. Thank you for your vision and dedication.

To my friend Jessica, who photographed a few of the images in this book at a time I never even thought publishing a book was possible, I am grateful.

To Lize and Emma: Thank you for helping Azure Farm run smoothly. I could not do it all without your help.

I am profoundly grateful to my dear friends who have known about this book project and offered their unwavering support, celebration, and encouragement along the way. Your belief in and continued championing of me strengthen and inspire me. I am truly blessed to have you by my side, and I cherish the friendship we share.

A heartfelt thank you to my editors, Thom and Meredith; art director, Hailey; and the rest of the team at Quarto. Your belief in the concept of this book and your dedicated efforts to bring it to life are so much appreciated. You saw the vision and championed me every step of the way.

To my social media family. Without you, this book would never have happened. Because of your support and love, I can do something I love each day and share it with the world. You have helped spread the name Azure Farm and I am so very grateful to each of you who watch, listen, support, comment, and share. You inspire me.

I thank God for creating this beautiful world full of flowers, animals, and plants for me to live in, and for giving me the desire to live a simple life and the courage to share it with others. Because of You, I stand boldly where I am today and am encouraged to share my truth with each seed I plant.

To everyone who reads this book, it is my desire that it leads you to a better life.

With heartfelt thanks,

ABOUT THE AUTHOR

ANNETTE THURMON is a modern-day homesteader who lives with her husband, Jared, and their daughter, Ava, in the small town of Adairsville, Georgia. After years of city life, Annette sought a simpler way of living and moved to the country. There, she cares for her organic garden and orchard and her animals, which include alpacas, miniature donkeys, chickens, turkeys, bees, and more! She is self-taught and loves sharing with others what she has learned over the years. She is the author of the children's book *Percy's Big Adventure* and the cookbook *The Harvest Table*.

Annette's goal is to inspire others to live a simple country lifestyle. She shares her daily adventures on social media, @azurefarm; her website, azurefarm.com; and the Azure Farm Podcast, which she co-hosts with her husband.

Index